Lizards

Lizards Pets Care, Beha

Costs and Health.

By

Ben Team

Table of Contents

Foreword

Modern reptile enthusiasts are fortunate to have the chance to keep a variety of different reptiles, ranging from colorful constricting snakes to gigantic tortoises. But there are likely more lizard species available than snakes, turtles, or crocodilians.

This is due in part to the simple fact that there are more lizard species in the world than any other type of (non-avian) reptile.

There are roughly 3,700 described snake species, 350-odd turtles and tortoises, and about 25 crocodilian species, depending on the authority consulted. But lizards form a much larger group; in total, they're represented by nearly 6,700 species.

However, the number of lizard species available to hobbyists is also influenced by demand. Importers and breeders only want to supply the market with species that hobbyists want to buy.

And because reptile enthusiasts have interest in a wide variety of lizard species, suppliers are eager to make them available on the market.

Additionally, and perhaps most importantly, many lizard species can thrive in captivity and make good pets. This includes species that are only suitable for experienced keepers, who've learned some of the finer points of lizard care, as well as fledgling keepers, who must learn everything about lizard-keeping from scratch.

We'll try to help lizard keepers at both ends of this spectrum in the following pages. We'll cover the basics of lizard care, including the best ways to house, feed, and maintain your new pet, but we'll also provide some advanced tips and tricks, that may even prove helpful for lizard-keeping veterans.

Just remember that lizard species differ in a variety of ways, so they'll all need different types of care. Accordingly, you'll need to be sure to not only learn about keeping lizards in general, but you'll need to learn some of the specific care requirements for your chosen species.

But you can begin learning about both in the following pages. With sufficient effort and dedication, you'll likely be successful maintaining your new pet and find the entire experience quite rewarding.

About the Author

The author, Ben Team, is an environmental educator and author with over 16 years of professional reptile-keeping experience.

Ben currently maintains www.FootstepsInTheForest.com, where he shares information, narration and observations of the natural world.

PART I: LIZARDS

Properly caring for any animal requires an understanding of the species and its place in the natural world. This includes digesting subjects as disparate as anatomy and ecology, diet and geography, and reproduction and physiology.

It is only by learning what your pet is, how it lives, what it does that you can achieve the primary goal of animal husbandry: Providing your pet with the highest quality of life possible.

Chapter 1: General Lizard Description and Anatomy

Most lizard species have evolved a number of morphological adaptations to help them survive. In some cases, these adaptations are subtle and similar to those found in other lizards, and in other cases, they are entirely unique to one.

Below, we'll discuss some of the primary physical characteristics of lizards.

Size

Lizards vary greatly in size; some measure only a few inches in length and weigh less than an ounce, while others approach 10 feet in length and weigh several hundred pounds.

However, there are a number of species that fall within the "sweet spot" for hobbyists – somewhere in the 1- to 2-foot-long (30 to 100 centimeter) range. Lizards of this size are large enough to feed, house and handle easily, while not being so large that they become dangerous.

Hatchlings often mirror the eventual adult size, as larger species generally produce larger young. Some of the smallest measure less than 4 inches (10 centimeters) upon hatching, while others may be nearly 1 foot long (30 centimeters) at the time of hatching or birth.

Scalation

As a group, lizards exhibit wildly varying scale patterns. Some have smooth, polished scales which lie flat against the animal's body, while others may be covered in various bumpy or wart-like scales. Some even feature hardened scales, which are almost armor-like in appearance.

In many cases, these different scale types and arrangements provide adaptive value – they help the lizard to survive.

For example, the polished scales of many sand-dwelling lizards allow the lizards to "swim" through the sand in their habitats. The rough, thick and armor-like scales of other species provide protection from predators or conspecifics.

Some other lizard species bear scales that help to change the animal's silhouette, thereby serving as a form of camouflage. Still others have scales that grow in unusual ways that presumably help the animal to discourage rivals or attract mates.

Color and Pattern

As a group, lizards come in just about every color of the rainbow. Many are black, brown, grey or earth-toned, but there are plenty of species clad in bold red, yellow, orange or green.

Many lean and quick lizard species tend to be unicolored or bear longitudinal stripes, while shorter, stouter lizards often bear horizontally oriented markings.

The former help make it more difficult for predators to track the escape attempts of quick lizards, while the latter help to camouflage lizards who are unlikely to be fast enough to evade predators.

Age-related color and pattern changes also occur in some species. This is perhaps exemplified best by Dumeril's monitors (*Varanus dumerilii*), who have bright yellow or red heads and bands when they hatch but become relatively drab grey or brown a short time later.

In addition to naturally occurring color variations, many pet species are also available with different genetic mutations that affect their color. For example, albino (amelanistic) forms occur in many species.

Body, Head and Tail

Lizards have wildly varying body shapes. Some are long and lean, while others are short and squat.

For example, many skinks, race runners and other fast lizards have long, skinny bodies. Meanwhile, several monitor species, some iguanas and a variety of other species have thick, powerful bodies, which don't allow for such quick movement.

The tail length of lizards also varies from one species to the next. Many climbing species have prehensile tails, while others have thick, bulbous tails which help store fat.

Other species rely on their tails for defense. Some lizards – including many iguanas and monitor lizards – will use their long tail as a whip. Others, such as uromastyx lizards, have club-like tails, covered in sharp scales.

The heads of most lizards are broadly similar in shape and relative size. However, they also vary in numerous ways based on the lizard's lifestyle. For example, the mouths of some snail-eating lizards are very robust, which allows them to crush their well-protected prey.

However, other species have relatively thin, pointy snouts, which allow them to better deal with small prey.

Vent

All lizards possess a vent at the base of their tail. Located on the ventral side of the body, the vent serves as the exit point for urates, feces and musk.

The vent is also the place from which the hemipenes of males and the eggs or young produced by females emerge.

Internal Organs

There are a relatively few internal anatomical differences between different lizard species.

Lizards draw oxygen in through their nostrils; pipe it through the trachea and into the lungs. Here, blood exchanges carbon dioxide for oxygen, before it is pumped to the various body parts via the heart and blood vessels.

While the hearts of lizards feature only three true chambers (two atria and a single ventricle), a septum keeps the ventricle divided at most times, allowing the heart to operate somewhat similarly to a four-chambered, mammalian heart.

This means that in practice, lizards keep their oxygenated and deoxygenated blood pretty separate in the heart.

Their digestive system is comprised of an esophagus, stomach, small intestine, large intestine and a terminal chamber called the cloaca. The stomach has some ability to stretch and accommodate food.

The liver resides near the center of the animal's torso, with the gallbladder sitting directly behind it. While the gallbladder stores bile, the liver provides a number of functions relating to digestion, metabolism and filtration.

Kidneys, which lie almost directly behind the lungs, filter wastes from the lizard's bloodstream.

Lizards control their bodies via the brain and nervous system. Their endocrine and exocrine glands work much as they do in other vertebrates.

Reproductive Organs

Like all squamates, male lizards have paired reproductive organs, called hemipenes. When not in use, males keep their hemipenes inside the bases of their tails. When they attempt to mate with a female, they evert one of the hemipenes and insert it into the female's cloaca.

The paired nature of the male sex organs ensures that males can continue to breed if they suffer an injury to one of the hemipenes. This paired arrangement also allows male lizards to mate with females on either side of their body.

Females have paired ovaries, which produce ova (eggs), and they have paired oviducts, which store the eggs after they are released from the ovaries.

Most lizards reproduce by laying eggs, but a small number of species give live birth. The eggs or young are held inside the oviducts until it is time to deposit them.

Chapter 2: General Lizard Biology and Behavior

Lizards vary significantly from one species to the next and exhibit a number of biological and behavioral adaptations that allow them to survive in their natural habitats.

However, there are a few behaviors and processes that are common to most species.

Shedding

Like other scaled reptiles, lizards periodically shed their old skin to reveal new, fresh skin underneath. Shedding may occur as often as every two to four weeks or as infrequently as twice as year. The rate at which a lizard sheds largely depends on its growth rate, although stress, illness and injury may also trigger rapid shed cycles.

Unlike snakes, who typically shed in one long, full piece, lizards usually shed in several large pieces. Most lizards exhibit their boldest coloration immediately following a shed.

Metabolism and Digestion

Lizards are ectothermic ("cold-blooded") animals, whose internal metabolism depends on their body temperature. When warm, their bodily functions proceed more rapidly; when cold, their bodily functions proceed slowly.

This also means that the lizards digest more effectively at suitably warm temperatures than they do at suboptimal temperatures. Their appetites also vary with temperature, and if the temperatures drop below the preferred range, they may cease feeding entirely.

A lizard's body temperature largely follows ambient air temperatures, but they also absorb and reflect radiant heat, such as that coming from the sun. Lizards try to keep their body temperature within the preferred range by employing behaviors that allow them to adjust their temperature.

For example, many lizards bask to raise their temperature when they are too cool. This typically involves orienting their body so that they are perpendicular to the sun's rays.

By contrast, when it is necessary to cool off, lizards may move into the shade or venture underground to escape the heat.

Growth Rate and Lifespan

Different lizards have different growth rates and lifespans, although there are some relatively broad trends among most pet species.

While most lizards will continue to grow throughout their lives, their growth rate slows significantly upon reaching maturity. Typically, lizards mature in about 1 to 5 years.

There is also a great deal of variation in *individual* growth rates – even among siblings in the same clutch. Some clutchmates will usually grow more quickly than their siblings will. This can lead some individuals to reach twice the size of their siblings within a few months' time.

Little is known about the lifespan of most lizard species, although all are probably capable of living longer in captivity – where they needn't fear predators and enjoy veterinary care – than they are in the wild.

Nevertheless, most commonly kept lizard species probably have average lifespans of 5 to 15 years, or perhaps a little longer. However, some of the largest species – including iguanas and monitor lizards -- can likely live longer than this.

Foraging Behavior

Lizards acquire food in one of two primary ways: They either forage actively for food, or remain in one location, and wait for prey to walk by.

Some species will use whichever approach is best-suited for the situation, while others generally stick to one approach over the other.

Generally speaking, most species who are capable of running at high speed tend to forage rather than wait in place for food to walk by. Skinks and teiids are great examples of species who primarily rely on foraging to acquire food.

On the other hand, many species who aren't capable of moving quickly – such as, most notably, true chameleons – are usually ambush hunters, who wait for food to come near them.

Diel and Seasonal Activity

Most lizards tend to be active during the day, but a small number of species – including many geckos -- sleep or rest during the day and emerge at night.

The former are called diurnal species, while the latter are referred to as nocturnal species. Those who are active at dawn and dusk are called crepuscular.

Lizards can only remain active during the times of year in which temperatures are suitably warm. This means that most species living in temperate areas become inactive and brumate during the winter. Conversely, those living in tropical areas often remain active all year long.

Similarly, some species aestivate during the summer, if the temperatures rise too high or the conditions become too dry.

Defensive Strategies and Tactics

As a group, lizards exhibit an array of defensive tactics.

Some of the defensive techniques lizards employ are widespread and occur across the entire group, while others are limited to a species or closely related group thereof.

For example, most lizards will attempt to use camouflage to avoid detection, and flee it discovered. However, there are some species for which one of these strategies is unlikely to prove helpful.

Additionally, most lizards will attempt to bite predators that grab them, and many will also defecate when grabbed by a predator to make them less appealing.

Many lizards will also autotomize their tails, but others will use their tails as a whip or club. Some have even evolved the ability to inflate their body, to prevent predators from being able to extricate them from rock crevices.

Many lizards are also capable of breathing loudly or making their bodies appear larger and more intimidating. Some species will also gape their mouths in response to a predator.

In captivity, some lizards continue to view their keeper as a potential threat for their entire lives, but others eventually learn that their keeper is not dangerous.

Reproduction

Different lizard species and populations exhibit varying reproductive timing.

However, most species commence breeding activities in the spring, as soon as temperatures are warm enough to permit normal activity.

Some individuals may continue to mate throughout the summer season, while others only breed for a narrow window of time. A few species instead exhibit a spring-and-fall breeding pattern.

Most females produce clutches or litters in the summer or fall, depending on the climate and typical mating season. The duration of pregnancy varies greatly between species, and to a lesser extent among individuals and different clutches or litters produced by a given female.

Chapter 3: Classification and Taxonomy

Like all other living creatures, lizards are placed within a hierarchical classification scheme. The highest levels of this classification scheme help distinguish groups like vertebrates from others, while the lower levels of classification distinguish individual species.

The general classification scheme for lizards is as follows:

Kingdom: Animalia
Phylum: Chordata
Class: Reptilia
Order: Squamata

All 6,000-odd described lizard species fit into the above hierarchy, but they are placed in a variety of different infraorders, families and genera.

There are five primary infraorders of lizards:

Anguimorpha
The infraorder Anguimorpha contains a large number of snake-like lizard species. A few of the most notable families contained within this infraorder include:

- Legless lizards (Family Anguidae)
- Beaded lizards and Gila monsters (Family Helodermatidae)
- Crocodile lizards (Family Shinisauridae)
- Earless monitor lizard (Family Lanthanotidae)
- Monitor lizards (Family Varanidae)

Gekkota
The infraorder Gekkota contains all of the living geckos, as as well as a few limbless lizards. Some of the most notable families in this group include:

- "Typical" geckos (Family Gekkonidae)
- Geckos with eyelids (Family Eublepharidae)
- Frog-eyed geckos and their relatives (Family Sphaerodactylidae)

Iguania

Iguania is a very diverse infraorder, which contains 14 different families. The species in this group run the gamut from tiny arboreal insectivores to large terrestrial herbivores. A few of the most notable families within the infraorder Iguania include:

- Iguanas (Family Iguanidae)
- Anoles (Family Dactyloidae)
- Agamids (Family Agamidae)
- Chameleons (Family Chamaeleonidae)

Lacertoidea

In contrast to many of the other lizard infraorders, Lacertoidea only contains a few families. Most members of this group have very smooth scales, and some have bifurcated tongues like snakes do. The principle families of the infraorder include:

- Lacertas and their relatives (Family Lacertidae)
- Tegus and their relatives (Family Teiidae)
- "Micro" teiids (Family Gymnophthalmidae)
- The (mostly) legless, burrowing amphisbaenians (Family Amphisbaenidae)

Scincomorpha

The infraorder Scincomorpha is primarily comprised of skinks – one of the most speciose lizard groups in the world – and some of their close relatives. A few of the most noteworthy families of the group include:

- Skinks (Family Scincidae)
- Girdled lizards (Family Cordylidae)
- Night lizards (Family Xantusiidae)

Note that, as with all other groups of living organisms, many scientists embrace differing taxonomic systems. So, you may see some of these families organized in different ways.

Chapter 4: The Lizard's World

All lizard species have evolved to live in a particular habitat (or collection of several different habitats). But some exhibit far greater specialization than others in this regard.

For example, green iguanas (*Iguana iguana*) range across a wide area and inhabit several different types of habitats. Conversely, some anoles (*Anolis* spp.) are very specialized for inhabiting a given portion of the tree canopy and only live on a single island.

To keep your lizard as healthy as possible, you'll want to provide him with a habitat that provides similar conditions to that which he would be exposed in the wild.

You'll primarily want to consider two key factors when doing so: The range and habitat your lizard prefers.

Range

Lizards range across most of the planet, save for the poles and a few islands. As with most other ectothermic animals, the greatest species richness is found close to the equator, while only a few species live at high latitudes.

Accordingly, it is difficult to make broad generalizations about the ecology of all 6,000-odd lizard species.

Nevertheless, you can generally assume that lizards hailing from tropical regions typically reach larger sizes than their close relatives who live in temperate regions. Tropical species also tend to remain active for a longer period of the year than lizards from temperate areas – who must cope with a long, cold winter season – are.

Generally speaking, species hailing from tropical regions are more commonly kept as pets by reptile enthusiasts. However, there are a few temperate species that make interesting pets.

Habitat

Lizards have managed to colonize just about every habitat type except for those found at extreme latitudes or altitudes. At least one species has even evolved to feed on algae growing in the ocean.

Generally speaking, lizards live in one of four broad habitat types: forest, grassland, desert or aquatic areas.

Forest-dwelling lizards tend to prefer relatively moderate temperatures and, often, dim lighting. They also prefer higher humidity levels than lizards living in open habitats.

Forest-dwelling lizards are obviously more likely to be arboreal than species living in treeless habitats. But that doesn't mean all lizards living in the forest climb trees, as many live their lives solely on the ground.

Lizards who live in deserts or grasslands share a number of similarities, although desert-dwellers possess adaptations that enable them to thrive in the relative humidity of the area (the difference in rainfall is the primary distinguishing feature between grasslands and deserts).

Many grassland or desert species require less drinking water than those living in forests or aquatic habitats. Some drink dew droplets off vegetation, while others obtain most of their water from their food.

Because these types of habitats are quite exposed to flying predators, most lizards living in grasslands and deserts spend a lot of time in rodent burrows, rock crevices and similar hiding places.

Lizards who prefer aquatic habitats are somewhat rare, and they all spend varying amounts of time in the water. Crocodile skinks (*Tribolonotus* spp.), water monitors (*Varanus salvator*), and basilisks (*Basiliscus* spp.) are some of the species that are most commonly associated with aquatic habitats. Unsurprisingly, all are accomplished swimmers.

Most lizards who live in or around aquatic habitats should be provided with a very large water dish in their habitat.

PART II: LIZARD HUSBANDRY

Once equipped with a basic understanding of what lizards *are* (Chapter 1 and Chapter 3), where they *live* (Chapter 4), and what they *do* (Chapter 2) you can begin learning about their captive care.

Animal husbandry is an evolving pursuit. Keepers shift their strategies frequently as they incorporate new information and ideas into their husbandry paradigms.

There are few "right" or "wrong" answers, and what works in one situation may not work in another. Accordingly, you may find that different authorities present different, and sometimes conflicting, information regarding the care of lizards.

In all cases, you must strive to learn as much as you can about your pet and its natural habitat, so that you may provide it with the best quality of life possible.

Chapter 5: Lizards as Pets

Lizards can make rewarding pets, but you must know what to expect before adding one to your home. This includes not only understanding the nature of the care they require but also the costs associated with this care.

Assuming that you feel confident in your ability to care for a lizard and endure the associated financial burdens, you can begin seeking your individual pet.

Understanding the Commitment

Keeping a lizard as a pet requires a substantial commitment. You will be responsible for your pet's well-being for the rest of its life.

Many lizard species live for at least 5 years, and some – including many monitor lizards and iguanas – may live for decades. You must be prepared to care for your new pet for this entire time.

Can you be sure that you will still want to care for your pet several years in the future? Do you know what your living situation will be? What changes will have occurred in your family? How will your working life have changed over this time?

You must consider all of these possibilities before acquiring a new pet. Failing to do so often leads to apathy, neglect and even resentment, which is not good for you or your pet lizard.

Neglecting your pet is wrong, and in some locations, a criminal offense. You must continue to provide quality care for your lizard, even once the novelty has worn off, and it is no longer fun to clean the cage and provide him with insects each week.

Once you purchase a lizard, its well-being becomes your responsibility until it passes away at the end of a long life, or you have found someone who will agree to adopt the animal for you. Unfortunately, this is rarely an easy task. You may begin with thoughts of selling your pet to help recoup a small part of your investment, but these efforts will largely fall flat.

While professional breeders may profit from the sale of lizards, amateurs are at a decided disadvantage. Only a tiny sliver of the general population is interested in reptilian pets, and only a small subset of these are interested in keeping lizards.

Of those who are interested in acquiring a lizard, most would rather start fresh, by *purchasing* a small hatchling or juvenile from an established breeder, rather than adopting your questionable animal *for free.*

After having difficulty finding a willing party to purchase or adopt your animal, many owners try to donate their pet to a local zoo. Unfortunately, this rarely works either.

Zoos are not interested in your lizard, no matter how pretty he is. He is a pet with little to no reliable provenance and questionable health status. This is simply not the type of animal zoos are eager to add to their multi-million-dollar collections.

Zoos obtain most of their animals from other zoos and museums; failing that, they obtain their animals directly from their land of origin. As a rule, they do not accept donated pets.

No matter how difficult it becomes to find a new home for your unwanted lizard, you must never release non-native reptiles into the wild.

Additionally, released or escaped reptiles cause a great deal of distress to those who are frightened by them. This leads local municipalities to adopt pet restrictions or ban reptile keeping entirely.

The Costs of Captivity

Reptiles are often marketed as low-cost pets. While true in a relative sense (the costs associated with dog, cat, horse or tropical fish husbandry are often much higher than they are for most lizards), potential keepers must still prepare for the financial implications of lizard ownership.

At the outset, you must budget for the acquisition of your pet, as well as the costs of purchasing or constructing a habitat. Unfortunately, while many keepers plan for these costs, they typically fail to consider the on-going costs, which will quickly eclipse the initial startup costs.

Startup Costs
One surprising fact most new keepers learn is the enclosure and equipment will often cost as much as (or more than) the animal does (except in the case of very high-priced specimens).

Prices fluctuate from one market to the next, but in general, the least you will spend on a healthy, captive-bred lizard is about $50 (£36); you'll also need to spend another $50 (£36) on his initial habitat and care equipment. Replacement equipment and food will represent additional (and ongoing) expenses.

Ongoing Costs
The ongoing costs of lizard ownership primarily fall into one of three categories: food, maintenance and veterinary care.

Food costs are the most significant of the three, but they are relatively consistent and somewhat predictable. Some maintenance costs are easy to calculate, but things like equipment malfunctions are impossible to predict with any certainty. Veterinary expenses are hard to predict and vary wildly from one year to the next.

Food Costs
Food is the single greatest ongoing cost you will experience while caring for your lizard. To obtain a reasonable estimate of your yearly food costs, you must consider the number of meals you will feed your pet per year and the cost of each meal.

The amount of food your lizard will consume will vary based on numerous factors, including his size, the average temperatures in his habitat and his health.

Veterinary Costs
While you should always seek veterinary advice at the first sign of illness, it is probably not wise to haul your healthy lizard to the vet's office for no reason – they don't require "checkups" or annual vaccinations as some other pets may. Accordingly, you shouldn't incur any veterinary expenses unless your pet falls ill.

However, veterinary care can become very expensive, very quickly. In addition to a basic exam or phone consultation, your lizard may need cultures, x-rays or other diagnostic tests performed. In light of this, wise keepers budget at least $200 to $300 (£160 to £245) each year to cover any emergency veterinary costs.

Maintenance Costs
It is important to plan for both routine and unexpected maintenance costs. Commonly used items, such as paper towels, disinfectant and topsoil are rather easy to calculate. However, it is not easy to know how many burned out light bulbs, cracked misting units or faulty thermostats you will have to replace in a given year.

Those who keep their lizard in simple enclosures will find that about $50 (£40) covers their yearly maintenance costs. By contrast, those who maintain elaborate habitats may spend $200 (£160) or more each year.

Always try to purchase frequently used supplies, such as light bulbs, paper towels and disinfectants in bulk to maximize your savings. It is often beneficial to consult with local reptile-keeping clubs, who often pool their resources to attain greater buying power.

Myths and Misunderstandings
Unfortunately, there are many myths and misunderstandings about lizards and reptile-keeping in general. Some myths represent outdated thinking or techniques, while other myths and misunderstandings reflect the desires of keepers, rather than the reality of the situation.

Myth: *Lizards will only grow to the size of their enclosure, and then they stop growing entirely.*

Fact: Despite the popularity of this myth, healthy lizards do not stop growing until they reach their mature, adult size. Keeping a lizard in an inappropriately small cage is an inhumane practice that will only lead to a stressed, sick animal.

Myth: *Lizards are reptiles, so they are not capable of suffering or feeling pain.*

Fact: While it is important to avoid anthropomorphizing or projecting human emotions and motivations to non-human entities, reptiles – including lizards – feel pain. There is no doubt that they can experience pain and seek to avoid it. While it is impossible to know exactly what a lizard thinks, there is no reason to believe that they do not suffer similarly to other animals, when injured, ill or depressed.

Myth: *My* lizard *likes to be held so he can feel the warmth of my hands.*

Fact: In truth, your lizard may tolerate being held, but it probably does not "like" it. This myth springs from the notion that because reptiles are "cold-blooded," and they must derive their heat from external sources, they must enjoy warmth at all times. However, this is an oversimplification of their behavior.

Myth: *Lizards are good pets for young children.*

Fact: While many reptiles, including lizards, make wonderful pets for adults, teenagers and families, they require more care than a young child can provide. The age at which a child is capable of caring for a pet will vary, but children should be about 10 to 12 years of age before they are allowed to care for their own lizard. Parents must exercise prudent judgment and make a sound assessment of their child's capabilities and maturity. Children will certainly enjoy pet reptiles, but they must be cared for by someone with adequate maturity. Additionally, it is important to consider the potential for young children contracting salmonella and other pathogens from the family pet.

Myth: *If you get tired of a lizard, it is easy to find a new home for it. The zoo will surely want your pet; after all, you are giving it to them free of charge! If that doesn't work, you can always just release it into the wild.*

Fact: Acquiring a pet lizard is a very big commitment. If you ever decide that your pet no longer fits your family or lifestyle, you may have a tough time finding a suitable home for it. You can attempt to sell the animal, but this is illegal in some places, and often requires a permit or license to do legally.

Zoos and pet stores will be reticent to accept your pet – even at no charge – because they cannot be sure that your pet does not have an illness that could spread through their collections. A zoo may have to spend hundreds or thousands of dollars for the care, housing and veterinary care to accept your pet lizard, and such things are not taken lightly.

Some people consider releasing their lizard into the wild if no other accommodations can be made, but such acts are destructive, often illegal and usually a death sentence for the lizard.

Even if you live within your lizard's natural range, captive animals should never be released into the wild, as they can spread pathogens that may wipe out a native population. You will likely have to solicit the help of a rescue group or shelter devoted to reptiles in finding a new home for an unwanted pet.

Acquiring Your Lizard

Modern reptile enthusiasts can acquire lizards from a variety of sources, each with a different set of pros and cons.

Pet stores are one of the first places many people see lizards offered for sale, and they become the de facto source of pets for many beginning keepers. While they do offer some unique benefits to prospective keepers, pet stores are not always the best place to purchase a pet lizard; so, consider all of the available options, including breeders and reptile swap meets, before making a purchase.

Pet Stores

Pet stores offer a number of benefits to keepers shopping for lizards, including convenience: They usually stock all of the equipment your new lizard needs, including cages, heating devices and food items.

Additionally, they offer you the chance to inspect the lizard up close before purchase. In some cases, you may be able to choose from more than one specimen. Many pet stores provide health guarantees for a short period, which provide some recourse if your new pet turns out to be ill.

However, pet stores are not always the ideal place to purchase your new lizard. Pet stores are retail establishments, and as such, you will usually pay more for your new pet than you would from a breeder.

Additionally, pet stores rarely know the pedigree of the animals they sell, and they will rarely know the lizard's date of birth or other pertinent information.

Other drawbacks associated with pet stores primarily relate to the staff's inexperience. While some pet stores concentrate on reptiles and may educate their staff about proper lizard care, many others provide incorrect advice to their customers.

It is also worth considering the increased exposure to pathogens that pet store animals endure, given the constant flow of animals through such facilities.

Reptile Expos
Reptile expos offer another option for purchasing lizards. Reptile expos often feature resellers, breeders and retailers in the same room, all selling various types of lizards and other reptiles.

Often, the prices at such events are quite reasonable and you are often able to select from many different lizards. However, if you have a problem, it may be difficult to find the seller after the event is over.

Breeders
Because they usually offer unparalleled information and support to their customers, breeders are generally the best place for most novices to shop for lizards. Additionally, breeders often know the species well and are better able to help you learn the husbandry techniques necessary for success.

The primary disadvantage of buying from a breeder is that you must often make such purchases from a distance, either by phone or via the internet. Nevertheless, most established breeders are happy to provide you with photographs of the animal you will be purchasing, as well as his or her parents.

Selecting Your Lizard

Not all lizards are created equally, so it is important to select a healthy individual that will give you the best chance of success.

Practically speaking, the most important criterion to consider is the health of the animal. However, the sex, age and history of the lizard are also important things to consider.

Health Checklist

Always check any lizard you are considering purchasing thoroughly for signs of injury or illness before making the purchase. If you are buying the animal from someone in a different part of the country, you must inspect it immediately upon delivery. Notify the seller promptly if the animal exhibits any health problems.

Avoid the temptation to acquire or accept a sick or injured animal in hopes of nursing him back to health. Not only are you likely to incur substantial veterinary costs while treating your new pet, you will likely fail in your attempts to restore the lizard to full health. Sick animals rarely recover in the hands of novices.

Additionally, by purchasing injured or diseased animals, you incentivize poor husbandry on the part of the retailer. If retailers lose money on sick or injured animals, they will take steps to avoid this eventuality, by acquiring healthier stock in the first place and providing better care for their charges.

As much as is possible, try to observe the following features:

- **Observe the animal's skin**. It should be free of lacerations and other damage. Pay special attention to those areas that frequently sustain damage, such as the tail, digits and the front of the face. A small cut or abrasion may be relatively easy to treat, but significant abrasions and cuts are likely to become infected and require significant treatment.

- **Gently check the animal's crevices and creases for mites and ticks**. Avoid purchasing any animal that has ectoparasites. Additionally, you should avoid purchasing any other animals from this source, as they are likely to harbor parasites as well.

- Examine the animal's eyes and nostrils. The eyes should not be sunken, and they should be free of discharge. The nostrils should be clear and dry – lizards with runny noses or those who blow bubbles are likely to be suffering from a respiratory infection.

- Gently palpate the animal and ensure no lumps or anomalies are apparent. Lumps in the muscles or abdominal cavity may indicate parasites, abscesses or tumors.

- Observe the animal's demeanor. Healthy lizards are aware of their environment and react to stimuli. When active, the animal should calmly explore his environment. Avoid lethargic animals, which do not appear alert.

- Check the animal's vent. The vent should be clean and free of smeared feces. Smeared feces can indicate parasites or bacterial infections.

The Age

Hatchling lizards are often fragile until they reach about a month or two of age. Before this, they are unlikely to thrive in the hands of beginning keepers.

Accordingly, most beginners should purchase two- or three-month-old juveniles, who have already become well established. Animals of this age tolerate the changes associated with a new home better than very young specimens do. Further, given their larger size, they will better tolerate temperature and humidity extremes than smaller animals will.

Bearded dragons are one of the best species for beginners.

The Sex

Unless you are attempting to breed lizards, you should select a male pet, as females are more likely to suffer from reproduction-related health problems than males are.

Some females will produce and deposit (infertile) egg clutches upon reaching maturity, whether they are housed with a male or not. While this is not necessarily problematic, novices can easily avoid this unnecessary complication by selecting males as pets.

Quarantine

Because new animals may have illnesses or parasites that could infect the rest of your collection, it is wise to quarantine all new acquisitions. This means that you should keep any new animal as separated from the rest of your pets as possible. Only once you have ensured that the new animal is healthy should you introduce it to the rest of your collection.

During the quarantine period, you should keep the new lizard in a simplified habitat, with a paper substrate, water bowl, several branches (if appropriate for the species), basking spot and a few hiding places. Keep the temperature and humidity at ideal levels.

It is wise to obtain fecal samples from your lizard during the quarantine period. You can take these samples to your veterinarian, who can check them for signs of internal parasites. A lways treat any existing parasite infestations before removing the animal from quarantine.

Always tend to quarantined animals last, as this reduces the chances of transmitting pathogens to your healthy animals. Do not wash quarantined water bowls or cage furniture with those belonging to your healthy animals. Whenever possible, use completely separate tools for quarantined animals and those that have been in your collection for some time.

Always be sure to wash your hands thoroughly after handling quarantined animals, their cages or their tools. Particularly careful keepers wear a smock or alternative clothing when handling quarantined animals.

Quarantine new acquisitions for a minimum of 30 days; 60 or 90 days is even better. Many zoos and professional breeders maintain 180- or 360-day-long quarantine periods.

Chapter 6: Providing the Captive Habitat

Providing your lizard with appropriate housing is and essential aspect of captive care. In essence, the habitat you provide to your lizard becomes his "world."

In "the old days," those inclined to keep lizards had few choices with regard to caging. The two primary options were to build a custom cage from scratch or construct a lid to use with a fish aquarium.

By contrast, modern hobbyists have a variety of options from which to choose. In addition to building custom cages or adapting aquaria, dozens of different cage styles are available – each with different pros and cons.

Dimensions

Throughout their lives, lizards need a cage large enough to lay comfortably, access a range of temperatures and allow for sufficient exercise.

A good rule of thumb is to ensure that the lizard (with tail) is no longer than ½ of the cage's perimeter.

Remember, this rule is a guideline for the *minimum* amount of space your lizard requires. Always strive to offer the largest cage that you reasonably can. While many keepers suggest that large cages are intimidating to lizards, the truth is subtler. Contrary to the popular notion, large cages – in and of themselves – do not cause lizards to experience stress.

Lizards live in habitats that exceed even the largest cages by several orders of magnitude. What lizards do not often do, however, is spend much time exposed. Large, barren cages that do not feature complex cage props and numerous hiding places may very well stress lizards. However, large, complex habitats afford more space for exercising and exploring in addition to allowing for the establishment of a superb thermal gradient.

In addition to total space, the layout of the cage is also important – rectangular cages are strongly preferable for a variety of reasons:

- They allow the keeper to establish more drastic heat gradients.

- Cages with one long direction allow your lizard to stretch out better than square cage do.

- Front opening cages are easier to maintain when the cages are rectangular, as you do not have to reach as far back into the cage to reach the back wall.

Security

While most commonly kept lizards are considered harmless animals, it is extremely important to consider cage security.

Never use a cage to house a lizard if you are not certain that it is escape proof. Additionally, be sure to inspect all cages regularly to catch problems (such as a fraying bit of screen or a loose door gasket) before they are large enough to permit the lizard to escape.

Aquariums

Aquariums are popular choices for lizard cages, largely because of their ubiquity. Virtually any pet store that carries lizards also stocks aquariums.

Aquariums can make suitable lizard cages, but they have a number of drawbacks. For starters, glass cages are hard to clean, and they are easy to break while you are carrying them around. Aquariums that are large are likely to be extremely heavy.

Aquariums are only enclosed on five sides, so keepers have to purchase or build a suitable lid for the enclosure. After-market screen tops are available, but often, they are not secure enough.

Commercial Cages

Commercially produced cages have a number of benefits over other enclosures. Commercial cages usually feature doors on the front of the cage, allowing them to provide better access than top-opening cages do. Additionally, bypass glass doors or framed, hinged doors are generally more secure than after-market screened lids (as are used on aquariums) are.

Additionally, plastic cages are usually produced in dimensions that make more sense for lizards, and often have features that aid in heating and lighting the cage.

Commercial cages can be made out of wood, metal, glass or other substances, but the majority are PVC or ABS plastic.

Commercial cages are available in two primary varieties: those that are molded from one piece of plastic and those that are assembled from several different sheets. Assembled cages are less expensive and easier to construct, but molded cages have few (if any) seems or cracks in which bacteria and other pathogens can hide.

Some cage manufacturers produce cages in multiple colors. White is probably the best color for novices, as it is easy to see dirt, mites and other small problems.

Black cages do not show dirt as well. This can be helpful for more experienced keepers who have developed proper hygiene techniques over time. Additionally, colorful lizards often look very sharp against black cage walls.

Plastic Storage Containers

Plastic storage containers, such as those used for shoes, sweaters or food, make suitable cages for lizards if they are customized to make them secure. The lids for plastic storage boxes are almost never secure enough to be used for lizards without the addition of supplemental security measures.

Hobbyists and breeders overcome this by incorporating Velcro straps, hardware latches or other strategies into plastic storage container cages. While these can be secure, you must be sure they are 100-percent escape-proof before placing a lizard in such cages.

The safest way to use plastic storage containers is with the use of a wooden or plastic rack. In such systems, often called "lidless" systems, the shelves of the rack form the top to the cage sitting below them. The gap between the top of the sides of the storage containers and the bottom of the shelves is usually very tight – approximately one-eighth inch or less.

When plastic containers are used, you must drill or melt numerous holes for air exchange. If you are using a lid, it is acceptable to place the holes in the lid; however, if you are using a lidless system, you will have to make the holes in the sides of the boxes.

All holes should be made from the inside towards the outside. This will help reduce the chances of leaving sharp edges inside the cage, which could cut the lizard.

Homemade Cages

For keepers with access to tools and the desire and skill to use them, it is possible to construct homemade cages. However, this is not recommended for novice keepers, who do not yet have experience keeping lizards.

A number of materials are suitable for cage construction, and each has different pros and cons. Wood is commonly used, but must be adequately sealed to avoid rotting, warping or absorbing offensive odors.

Plastic sheeting is a very good material, but few have the necessary skills, knowledge and tools necessary for cage construction. Additionally, some plastics may have extended off-gassing times.

Glass can be used, whether glued to itself or with used with a frame. Custom-built glass cages can be better than aquariums, as you can design them in dimensions that are appropriate for lizards. Additionally, they can be constructed in such a way that the door is on the front of the cage, rather than the top.

Screen Cages

Screen cages make excellent habitats for some lizards, but they don't work well for others. Typically, screen enclosures are most commonly used with chameleons, as they require significant amounts of air exchange.

However, they're also used for some lizards (such as basilisks), which have a habit of running into the walls of their enclosures. So, by using a screened enclosure, keepers of these lizards can help prevent injuries.

Note that screen enclosures do not retain heat or humidity well, so keepers will have to adjust their maintenance practices to compensate.

Chapter 7: Heating the Habitat

Providing the proper thermal environment is one of the most important aspects of reptile husbandry. As ectothermic ("cold-blooded") animals, lizards rely on the surrounding temperatures to regulate the rate at which their metabolism operates.

Providing a proper thermal environment can mean the difference between a healthy, thriving pet and one who spends a great deal of time at the veterinarian's office, battling infections and illness.

While individuals may demonstrate slightly different preferences, and different species have slightly different preferences, most active lizards prefer ambient temperatures in the low-80s Fahrenheit (between 26 and 29 degrees Celsius). Inactive (sleeping) lizards prefer temperatures in the low 70s Fahrenheit (21 to 23 degrees Celsius).

However, while these are appropriate air temperatures for most lizards, they will also require a very warm basking spot during the day, with a temperature of at least 90 to 95 degrees Fahrenheit (32 to 35 degrees Celsius). Some desert-dwelling species require even warmer basking spots.

Providing your lizard with a suitable thermal environment requires the correct approach, the correct heating equipment and the tools necessary for monitoring the thermal environment.

Size-Related Heating Concerns
Before examining the best way to establish a proper thermal environment, it is important to understand that your lizard's body size influences the way in which he heats up and cools off.

Because volume increases more quickly than surface area does with increasing body size, small individuals experience more rapid temperature fluctuations than larger individuals do.

Accordingly, it is imperative to protect small individuals from temperature extremes. Conversely, larger lizards are more tolerant of temperature extremes than smaller individuals are (though they should still be protected from temperature extremes).

Thermal Gradients

In the wild, most lizards move between different microhabitats so that they can maintain ideal body temperature as much as possible.

The best way to do this is by clustering the heating devices at one end of the habitat, thereby creating a basking spot (the warmest spot in the enclosure).

The temperatures will slowly drop with increasing distance from the basking spot, which creates a *gradient* of temperatures. Barriers, such as branches and vegetation, also help to create shaded patches, which provide additional thermal options.

This mimics the way temperatures vary from one small place to the next in your pet's natural habitat. For example, a wild lizard may move under some vegetation to cool off at midday or move onto a sun-bathed branch to warm up in the morning.

By establishing a gradient in the enclosure, your captive lizard will be able to access a range of different temperatures, which will allow him to manage his body temperature just as his wild counterparts do.

Adjust the heating device until the surface temperatures at the basking spot are between 90- and 95-degrees Fahrenheit (32 to 35 degrees Celsius). Provide a slightly cooler basking spot for immature individuals, with maximum temperatures of about 90 degrees Fahrenheit (32 degrees Celsius).

Again, this is the proper temperature range for *many* lizard species, but some may require warmer basking spots.

Because there is no heat source at the other end of the cage, the ambient temperature will gradually fall as your lizard moves away from the heat source. Ideally, the cool end of the cage should be in the low 70s Fahrenheit (22 degrees Celsius).

The need to establish a thermal gradient is one of the most compelling reasons to use a roomy cage. In general, the larger the cage, the easier it is to establish a suitable thermal gradient.

Heating Equipment

There are a variety of different heating devices you can use to keep your lizard's habitat within the appropriate temperature range.

Be sure to consider your choice carefully and select the best type of heating device for you and your pet.

Heat Lamps

Heat lamps are usually the best choice for supplying heat to your lizard's habitat. Heat lamps consist of a reflector dome and an incandescent bulb. The light bulb produces heat (in addition to light) and the metal reflector dome directs the heat to a spot inside the cage.

You will need to clamp the lamp to a stable anchor or part of the cage's frame. Always be sure that the lamp is securely attached and will not be dislodged by vibration, children or pets.

Because fire safety is always a concern, and many keepers use high-wattage light bulbs, opt for heavy-duty reflector domes with ceramic bases, rather than economy units with plastic bases. The price difference is negligible, given the stakes.

One of the greatest benefits of using heat lamps to maintain the temperature of your pet's habitat is the flexibility they offer. While you can adjust the amount of heat provided by heat tapes and other devices with a rheostat or thermostat, you can adjust the enclosure temperature provided by heat lamps in two ways:

- Changing the Bulb Wattage

The simplest way to adjust the temperature of your pet's cage is by changing the wattage of the bulb you are using.

For example, if a 40-watt light bulb is not raising the temperature of the basking spot high enough, you may try a 60-watt bulb. Alternatively, if a 100-watt light bulb is elevating the cage temperatures higher than are appropriate, switching to a 60-watt bulb may help.

- Adjusting the Distance between the Heat Lamp and the Basking Spot

The closer the heat lamp is to the cage, the warmer the cage will be. If the habitat is too warm, you can move the light farther from the enclosure, which should lower the basking spot temperatures slightly.

However, the farther away you move the lamp, the larger the basking spot becomes. It is important to be careful that you do not move it too far away, which will reduce the effectiveness of the thermal gradient by heating the enclosure too uniformly. In very large cages, this may not compromise the thermal gradient very much, but in a small cage, it may eliminate the "cool side" of the habitat.

In other words, if your heat lamp creates a basking spot that is roughly 1-foot in diameter when it is 1 inch away from the screen, it will produce a slightly cooler, but larger basking spot when moved back another 6 inches or so.

Ceramic Heat Emitters

Ceramic heat emitters are small inserts that function similarly to light bulbs, except that they do not produce any visible light – they only produce heat.

Ceramic heat emitters are used in reflector-dome fixtures, just as heat lamps are. The benefits of such devices are numerous:

- They typically last much longer than light bulbs do

- They are suitable for use with thermostats

- They allow for the creation of overhead basking spots, as lights do

- They can be used day or night

However, the devices do have three primary drawbacks:

- They are very hot when in operation

- They are much more expensive than light bulbs

- You cannot tell by looking if they are hot or cool. This can be a safety hazard – touching a ceramic heat emitter while it is hot is likely to cause serious burns.

Radiant Heat Panels
Quality radiant heat panels are a great choice for heating most reptile habitats, including those containing lizards. Radiant heat panels are essentially heat pads that stick to the roof of the habitat. They usually feature rugged, plastic or metal casings and internal reflectors to direct the infrared heat back into the cage.

Radiant heat panels have a number of benefits over traditional heat lamps and under tank heat pads:

- They do not produce visible light, which means they are useful for both diurnal and nocturnal heat production. They can be used in conjunction with fluorescent light fixtures during the day and remain on at night once the lights go off.

- They are inherently flexible. Unlike many devices that do not work well with pulse-proportional thermostats, most radiant heat panels work well with on-off and pulse-proportional thermostats.

The only real drawback to radiant heat panels is their cost: radiant heat panels often cost about two to three times the price of light- or heat pad-oriented systems. However, many radiant heat panels outlast light bulbs and heat pads, a fact that offsets their high initial cost over the long term.

Heat Pads
Heat pads are an attractive option for many new keepers, but they are not without drawbacks.

- Heat pads have a high risk of causing contact burns.

- If they malfunction, they can damage the cage as well as the surface on which they are placed.

- They are more likely to cause a fire than heat lamps or radiant heat panels are.

However, if installed properly (which includes allowing fresh air to flow over the exposed side of the heat pad) and used in conjunction with a thermostat, they can be reasonably safe. With heat pads, it behooves the keeper to purchase premium products, despite the small increase in price.

Heat Tape

Heat tape is somewhat akin to a "stripped down" heat pad. In fact, most heat pads are simply pieces of heat tape that have already been connected and sealed inside a plastic envelope.

Heat tape is primarily used to heat large numbers of cages simultaneously. It is generally inappropriate for novices and requires the keeper to make electrical connections. Additionally, a thermostat is always required when using heat tape.

Historically, heat tape was used to keep water pipes from freezing – not to heat reptile cages. While some commercial heat tapes have been designed specifically for reptiles, many have not. Accordingly, it may be illegal, not to mention dangerous, to use heat tapes for purposes other than for which they are designed.

Heat Cables

Heat cables are similar to heat tape, in that they heat a long strip of the cage, but they are much more flexible to use. Many heat cables are suitable to use inside the cage, while others are designed for use outside the habitat.

Always be sure to purchase heat cables that are designed to be used in reptile cages. Those sold at hardware stores are not appropriate for use in a cage.

Heat cables must be used in conjunction with a thermostat, or, at the very least, a rheostat.

Nocturnal Temperatures

Because most lizards easily tolerate temperatures in the low-70s Fahrenheit (21 to 22 degrees Celsius) at night, most keepers can allow their pet's habitat to fall to ambient room temperature at night.

Because it is important to avoid using lights on your lizard's habitat at night, those living in homes with lower nighttime temperatures will need to employ additional heat sources. Most such keepers accomplish this through the use of ceramic heat emitters.

Thermometers

It is important to monitor the cage temperatures very carefully to ensure your pet stays healthy. Just as a water test kit is an aquarist's best friend, quality thermometers are some of the most important husbandry tools for reptile keepers.

Ambient and Surface Temperatures

Two different types of temperature are relevant for pet lizards: ambient temperatures and surface temperatures.

The ambient temperature in your animal's enclosure is the air temperature; the surface temperatures are the temperatures of the objects in the cage. Both are important to monitor, as they can differ widely.

Measure the cage's ambient temperatures with a digital thermometer. An indoor-outdoor model will feature a probe that allows you to measure the temperature at both ends of the thermal gradient at once. For example, you may position the thermometer at the cool side of the cage but attach the remote probe to a branch near the basking spot.

Because standard digital thermometers do not measure surface temperatures well, use a non-contact, infrared thermometer for such measurements. These devices will allow you to measure surface temperatures accurately from a short distance away.

Thermostats and Rheostats

Some heating devices, such as heat lamps, are designed to operate at full capacity for the entire time that they are turned on. Such devices should not be used with thermostats – instead, care should be taken to calibrate the proper temperature by tweaking the bulb wattage.

Other devices, such as heat pads, heat tape and radiant heat panels are designed to be used with a regulating device, such as a thermostat or rheostat, which maintains the proper temperature

Rheostats

Rheostats are similar to light-dimmer switches, and they allow you to reduce the output of a heating device. In this way, you can dial in the proper temperature for the habitat.

The drawback to rheostats is that they only regulate the amount of power going to the device – they do not monitor the cage temperature or adjust the power flow automatically. In practice, even with the same level of power entering the device, the amount of heat generated by most heat sources will vary over the course of the day.

If you set the rheostat so that it keeps the cage at the right temperature in the morning, it may become too hot by the middle of the day. Conversely, setting the proper temperature during the middle of the day may leave the morning temperatures too cool.

Care must be taken to ensure that the rheostat controller is not inadvertently bumped or jostled, causing the temperature to rise or fall outside of healthy parameters.

Thermostats

Thermostats are similar to rheostats, except that they also feature a temperature probe that monitors the temperature in the cage (or under the basking source). This allows the thermostat to adjust the power going to the device as necessary to maintain a predetermined temperature.

For example, if you place the temperature probe under a basking spot powered by a radiant heat panel, the thermostat will keep the temperature relatively constant at the basking site.

There are two different types of thermostats:

- On-Off Thermostats

On-Off Thermostats work by cutting the power to the device when the probe's temperature reaches a given temperature. For example, if the thermostat were set to 85 degrees Fahrenheit (29 degrees Celsius), the heating device would turn off whenever the temperature exceeds this threshold. When the temperature falls below 85, the thermostat restores power to the unit, and the heater begins functioning again. This cycle will continue to repeat, thus maintaining the temperature within a relatively small range.

Be aware that on-off thermostats have a "lag" factor, meaning that they do not turn off when the temperature reaches a given temperature. They turn off when the temperature is a few degrees above that temperature, and then turn back on when the temperate is a little below the set point. Because of this, it is important to avoid setting the temperature at the limits of your pet's acceptable range. Some premium models have an adjustable amount of threshold for this factor, which is helpful.

- Pulse Proportional Thermostats

Pulse proportional thermostats work by constantly sending pulses of electricity to the heater. By varying the rate of pulses, the amount of energy reaching the heating devices varies. A small computer inside the thermostat adjusts this rate to match the set-point temperature as measured by the probe. Accordingly, pulse proportional thermostats maintain much more consistent temperatures than on-off thermostats do.

Lights should not be used with thermostats, as the constant flickering may stress your pet. Conversely, heat pads, heat tape, radiant heat panels and ceramic heat emitters should always be used with either a rheostat or, preferably, a thermostat to avoid overheating your pet.

Thermostat Failure

If used for long enough, all thermostats eventually fail. The question is will yours fail today or twenty years from now. While some thermostats fail in the "off" position, a thermostat that fails in the "on" position may overheat your lizard. Unfortunately, tales of entire collections being lost to a faulty thermostat are too common.

Accordingly, it behooves the keeper to acquire high-quality thermostats. Some keepers use two thermostats, connected in a series arrangement. By setting the second thermostat (the "backup thermostat") a few degrees higher than the setting used on the "primary thermostat," you safeguard yourself against the failure of either unit.

In such a scenario, the backup thermostat allows the full power coming to it to travel through to the heating device, as the temperature never reaches its higher set-point temperature.

Leopard geckos are relatively easy for novices to maintain.

However, if the first unit fails in the "on" position, the second thermostat will keep the temperatures from rising too high. The temperature will rise a few degrees in accordance with the higher set-point temperature, but it will not get hot enough to harm your pets.

If the backup thermostat fails in the "on" position, the first thermostat retains control. If either fails in the "off" position, the temperature will fall until you rectify the situation, but a brief exposure to relatively cool temperatures is unlikely to be fatal.

Chapter 8: Lighting the Habitat

Given the amount of time some species spend hanging out in the sun, it should come as no surprise that many lizards have evolved to depend upon it.

It is always preferable to afford captive lizards access to unfiltered sunlight, but this is not always possible. In these cases, it is necessary to provide your lizard with high quality lighting, which can partially satisfy their need for real sunlight.

Lizards deprived of appropriate lighting may become seriously ill. Learning how to provide the proper lighting for reptiles is sometimes an arduous task for beginners, but it is very important to the long-term health of your pet that you do. To understand the type of light your lizard needs, you must first understand a little bit about light.

Lighting Basics for Lizard Keepers
Light is a type of energy that physicists call electromagnetic radiation; it travels in waves. These waves may differ in amplitude, which correlates to the vertical distance between consecutive wave crests and troughs, frequency, which correlates with the number of crests per unit of time, and wavelength.

Wavelength is the distance from one crest to the next, or one trough to the next. Wavelength and frequency are inversely proportional, meaning that as the wavelength increases, the frequency decreases. It is more common for reptile keepers to discuss wavelengths rather than frequencies.

The sun produces energy (light) with a very wide range of constituent wavelengths. Some of these wavelengths fall within a range called the visible spectrum; humans can detect these rays with their eyes. Such waves have wavelengths between about 390 and 700 nanometers. Rays with wavelengths longer or shorter than these limits are broken into their own groups and given different names.

Those rays with around 390 nanometer wavelengths or less are called ultraviolet rays or UV rays. UV rays are broken down into three different categories, just as the different colors correspond with different wavelengths of visible light. UVA rays have wavelengths between 315 to 400 nanometers, while UVB rays have wavelengths between 280 and 315 nanometers while UVC rays have wavelengths between 100 and 280 nanometers.

Rays with wavelengths of less than 280 nanometers are called x-rays and gamma rays. At the other end of the spectrum, infrared rays have wavelengths longer than 700 nanometers; microwaves and radio waves are even longer.

UVA rays are important for food recognition, appetite, activity and eliciting natural behaviors. UVB rays are necessary for many reptiles to produce vitamin D3. Without this vitamin, reptiles cannot properly metabolize their calcium.

The light that comes from the sun and light bulbs is composed of a combination of wavelengths, which create the blended white light that you perceive. This combination of wavelengths varies slightly from one light source to the next.

The sun produces very balanced white light, while "economy" incandescent bulbs produce relatively fewer blue rays and yields a yellow-looking light. High-quality bulbs designed for reptiles often produce very balanced, white light. The degree to which light causes objects to look as they would under sunlight is called the Color Rendering Index, or CRI. Sunlight has a CRI of 100, while quality bulbs have CRIs of 80 to 90; by contrast, a typical incandescent bulb has a CRI of 40 to 50

Another important characteristic of light that relates to chameleons is luminosity, or the brightness of light. Measured in units called Lux, luminosity is an important consideration for your lighting system. While you cannot possibly replicate the intensity of the sun's light, it is desirable in most circumstances to ensure the habitat is lit as well as is reasonably possible.

For example, in the tropics, the sunlight intensity averages around 100,000 Lux at midday; by comparison, the lights in a typical family living room only produce about 50 Lux.

Without bright lighting, many reptiles become lethargic, depressed or exhibit hibernating behaviors. Dim lighting may inhibit feeding and cause lizards to become stressed and ill.

To summarize, many lizards require:

- Light that is comprised of visible light, as well as UVA and UVB wavelengths

- Light with a high color-rendering index

- Light of the sufficiently strong intensity

Now that you know what your lizard requires, you can go about designing the lighting system for his habitat. Ultraviolet radiation is the most difficult component of proper lighting to provide, so it makes sense to begin by examining the types of bulbs that produce UV radiation.

The only commercially produced bulbs that produce significant amounts of UVA and UVB and suitable for a lizard habitat are linear fluorescent light bulbs, compact fluorescent light bulbs and mercury vapor bulbs.

Neither type of fluorescent bulb produces significant amounts of heat, but mercury vapor bulbs produce a lot of heat and serve a dual function. In many cases, keepers elect to use both types of lights – a mercury vapor bulb for a warm basking site with high levels of UV radiation and fluorescent bulbs to light the rest of the cage without raising the temperature. You can also use fluorescent bulbs to provide the requisite UV radiation and use a regular incandescent bulb to generate the basking spot.

Fluorescent bulbs have a much longer history of use than mercury vapor bulbs, which makes some keepers more comfortable using them. However, many models only produce moderate amounts of UVB radiation. While some mercury vapor bulbs produce significant quantities of UVB, some question the wisdom of producing more UV radiation than the animal receives in the wild. Additionally, mercury vapor bulbs are much too powerful to use in small habitats, and they are more expensive initially.

Most fluorescent bulbs must be placed within 12 inches of the basking surface, while some mercury vapor bulbs should be placed farther away from the basking surface – be sure to read the manufacturer's instructions before use. Be sure that the bulbs you purchase specifically state the amount of UVB radiation they produce; this figure is expressed as a percentage, for example 7% UVB. Most UVB-producing bulbs require replacement every six to 12 months – whether or not they have stopped producing light.

However, ultraviolet radiation is only one of the characteristics that lizard keepers must consider. The light bulbs used must also produce a sunlight-like spectrum. Fortunately, most high-quality light bulbs that produce significant amounts of UVA and UVB radiation also feature a high color-rendering index. The higher the CRI, the better, but any bulbs with a CRI of 90 or above will work well. If you are having trouble deciding between two otherwise evenly matched bulbs, select the one with the higher CRI value.

Brightness is the final, and easiest, consideration for the keeper to address. While no one yet knows what the ideal luminosity for a chameleon's cage, it makes sense to ensure that at least part of the cage features very bright lighting. However, you should always offer a shaded retreat within the enclosure into which your lizard can avoid the light if he desires.

Connect the lights to an electric timer to keep the length of the day and night consistent. Some breeders manipulate their captive's photoperiod over the course of the year to prime the animals for breeding, but pet chameleons thrive with 12 hours of daylight and 12 hours of darkness all year long.

Chapter 9: Enclosure Furniture

Strictly speaking, it is possible to keep most lizards in a cage devoid of anything but a substrate that permits burrowing and a water bowl. However, it is wise to provide most lizards with complex environments, containing numerous climbing opportunities in the cage – especially if you are keeping an arboreal species, who spends most of its time in the trees.

Additionally, many keepers enjoy decorating the cage to resemble the animal's natural habitat. While such measures are not necessary from the lizard's point of view, if implemented with care, there is no reason not to decorate your pet's cage, if you are inclined to do so.

However, it is recommended that beginners use a simple cage design for their first 6 to 12 months while they learn to provide effective husbandry.

Lizards will move about to find water, food, mates or appropriate environmental conditions. Each species (and individual) has a different typical activity level. Some may be accustomed to traveling many miles each day in search of food, but other lizards travel relatively little.

Hide Boxes

"Hide boxes" come in a wide variety of shapes, sizes and styles. Some keepers use modified plastic or cardboard containers, while others use realistic looking logs and wood pieces. Both approaches are acceptable, but all hides must offer a few key things:

- Hides should be safe for the lizard and feature no sharp edges or toxic chemicals.

- Hides should accommodate the lizard, but not much else. They should be only slightly larger than the animal's body when it is inside.

- Hides should have low profiles. Lizards prefer to feel the top of the hide contacting the dorsal surface of their body.

- Hides either must be easy and economical to replace or constructed from materials that are easy to clean.

Plastic Storage Boxes
Just as a plastic storage box can be converted into an acceptable enclosure, small storage boxes can be converted into functional hiding places. Food containers, shoeboxes and butter tubs can serve as the base.

If the container has a low profile, it needs only have a door cut into the tub. Alternatively, you can discard the lid, flip the tub upside down and cut an entrance hole in the side.

Plant Saucers
The saucers designed to collect the water that overfills potted plants make excellent hiding locations. All you have to do is flip them upside down and cut a small opening in the side for a door.

Clay or plastic saucers can be used, but clay saucers are hard to cut. If you punch an entrance hole into a clay saucer, you must sand or grind down the edges to prevent hurting your lizard.

Plates
Plastic, paper or ceramic plates make good hiding locations in cages that use particulate substrates. This will allow the lizard to burrow up under the plate through the substrate and hide in a very tight space. Such hiding places also make it very easy to access your lizard while he is hiding.

Cardboard Boxes
While you must discard and replace them anytime they become soiled, small cardboard boxes can also make suitable hide boxes. Just cut a hole in the side to provide a door.

Commercial "Half-Logs"
Many pet stores sell U-shaped pieces of wood that resemble half of a hollow log. While these are sometimes attractive looking items, they are not appropriate hide spots when used as intended.

The U-shaped construction means that the lizard will not feel the top of the hide when he is laying inside. These hides can be functional if they are partially buried, thus reducing the height of the hide.

Cork Bark

Real bark cut from the cork oak (*Quercus suber*), "cork bark" is a wonderful looking decorative item that can be implemented in a variety of ways.

Usually cork bark is available in tube shape or in flat sheets. Flat pieces should only be used with particulate, rather than sheet-like substrates so that the lizard can get under them easily.

Cork bark may be slightly difficult to clean, as its surface contains numerous indentations and crevices. Use hot water, soap and a sturdy brush to clean the pieces.

Commercially Produced Plastic Hides

Many different manufacturers market simple, plastic, hiding boxes. These are very functional if sized correctly, although some brands tend to be too tall. The simple design and plastic construction make them very easy to clean.

Paper Towel Tubes

Small sections of paper towel tubes make suitable hiding spots for small lizards. They do not last very long, so they require frequent replacement. They often work best if flattened slightly.

Newspaper or Paper Towels

Several sheets of newspaper or paper towels placed on top of the substrate (whether sheet-like or particulate) make suitable hiding spots.

Many professional breeders use paper-hiding spaces because it is such a simple and economically feasible solution. Some keepers crumple a few of the sheets to give the stack of paper more height.

Unusual Items

Some keepers like to express their individuality by using unique or unusual items as hiding spots. Some have used handmade ceramic items, while others have used skulls or turtle shells. If the four primary criteria previously discussed are met, there is no reason such items will not make suitable hiding spaces.

Humid Hides

In addition to security, lizards also derive another benefit from many of their hiding spaces in the wild. Most hiding places feature higher humidity than the surrounding air.

By spending a lot of time in such places, lizards are able to avoid dehydration in habitats where water is scarce. Additionally, sleeping in these humid retreats aids in the shedding process. You should take steps to provide similar opportunities in captivity.

Humid hides can be made by placing damp sphagnum moss in a plastic container. The moss should not be saturated, but merely damp. You can also use damp paper towels or newspaper to increase the humidity of a hide box.

Some keepers prefer to keep humid hides in the habitat at all times, while others use them periodically – usually preceding shed cycles. Humid hides should never be the only hides available to the lizard. Always use them in addition to dry hides.

Climbing Branches

It is important to provide arboreal lizards with climbing branches, so that they can exhibit their full range of natural behaviors.

Note that some lizards want large, thick branches, while others will prefer, thin branches, such as those found at the distal ends of the tree's canopy.

These types of branches can often be rested against the side of the habitat and may not need to be permanently affixed to the cage walls. Just be sure that the branch will support the weight of the lizard – you don't want your pet to fall and injure himself.

Note that while they are not strictly necessary, branches with leaves are preferable to barren branches, as they'll provide additional security for the lizard. The leaves will also provide shade and surfaces from which the lizard can drink droplets of water.

Many keepers find it helpful to routinely replace these branches as the leaves die and fall away. However, you can also intertwine artificial plants and vines or living, potted vines around the branches. This will alleviate the need to replace the branches periodically.

Some keepers instead place shrub-like plants inside the habitat to provide their lizard with climbing opportunities. This can be a good option, although there aren't many plants that provide suitable climbing opportunities and thrive in the relatively dim light of most enclosures.

Chapter 10: Substrates

Substrates are used to give your lizard a comfortable surface on which to dwell and to absorb any liquids present. There are a variety of acceptable choices, all of which have benefits and drawbacks. The only common substrate that is never acceptable is cedar shavings, which emits fumes that are toxic to lizards.

Paper Products
The easiest and safest substrates for most lizards are paper products in sheet form. While regular newspaper is the most common choice, some keepers prefer paper towels, unprinted newspaper, butcher's paper or a commercial version of these products.

Paper substrates are very easy to maintain, but they do not last very long and must be completely replaced when they are soiled. Accordingly, they must be changed regularly -- at least once per week.

Use several layers of paper products to provide sufficient absorbency and a little bit of cushion for the lizard.

Many pet stores and pet supply retailers now carry recycled paper pulp products that can be used as bedding. Many keepers have used these substrates successfully, but they don't offer the primary benefits that sheet-style paper products do.

For example, they're not as easy to replace and they represent an ingestion hazard. They also cost significantly more than a few sheets of newspaper, so they haven't become as popular as some keepers predicted.

Aspen
Shredded aspen bark is a popular substrate choice that works very well. Aspen shares most of the concerns that other particulate substrates do (ingestion hazards, increased labor), but it is a popular choice among many lizard keepers.

Aspen can be dusty, so look for brands that are advertised as "low dust." Aspen does not resist decay well, and you must keep it rather dry. This can be a problem for some lizard enclosures, which must be misted daily.

Aspen can be spot cleaned daily, but like most other particulate substrates, you must replace it completely every month.

Pine

Some hobbyists eschew pine, which is sometimes though to produce irritating fumes. While this may be true of products made from the xylem (wood) of pine trees, it is not true of products made from the bark.

Pine bark is not very absorbent, but it resists decay reasonably well. Pine bark is attractive and natural looking, but it does leave copious amounts of black dust inside the cage.

It can be spot cleaned daily but requires monthly replacement.

Orchid Bark

The bark of fir trees is often used for orchid propagation, and so it is often called "orchid bark." Orchid bark is very attractive, though not quite as natural looking as pine bark. However, it exceeds pine in most other ways except cost. Because orchid bark is often reddish in color, it is very easy to spot clean. However, monthly replacement can be expensive for those living in the eastern United States and Europe.

Cypress Mulch

Cypress mulch is a popular substrate choice for many tropical species, and it helps to provide a moderately high humidity level, which is often beneficial for many lizards.

One significant drawback to cypress mulch is that some brands (or individual bags among otherwise good brands) produce a stick-like mulch, rather than mulch composed of thicker pieces.

These sharp sticks can injure the keeper and the kept. It usually only takes one cypress mulch splinter jammed under a keeper's fingernail to cause them to switch substrates.

Soil

Organic potting soil or soil collected from a forested area can also be used in your lizard's enclosure. Both substrates are easy to acquire, affordable (or free) and retain moisture well, so they make excellent options.

Just be sure to collect the soil from an area that hasn't been exposed to pesticides or other chemicals, or, if you are purchasing the soil, opt for a variety that does not include perlite, fertilizers or other additives.

Chapter 11: Maintaining the Captive Habitat

Now that you have acquired your lizard and set up the enclosure, you must develop a protocol for maintaining his habitat. While lizard habitats require major maintenance every month or so, they only require minor daily maintenance.

In addition to designing a husbandry protocol, you must embrace a record-keeping system to track your lizard's growth and health.

Cleaning and Maintenance Procedures

Once you have decided on the proper enclosure for your pet, you must keep your lizard fed, hydrated and ensure that the habitat stays in proper working order to keep your captive healthy and comfortable.

Some tasks must be completed each day, while others should be performed weekly, monthly or annually.

Daily

- Monitor the ambient and surface temperatures of the habitat.

- Spot clean the cage to remove any feces, urates or pieces of shed skin in the enclosure.

- Ensure that the lights, latches and other moving parts are in working order.

- Verify that your lizard is acting normally and appears healthy. You do not necessarily need to handle him to do so.

Weekly

- Change sheet-like substrates (newspaper, paper towels, etc.).

- Clean the inside surfaces of the enclosure.

- Inspect your lizard closely for any signs of injury, parasites or illness.

- Wash and sterilize all food dishes.

Monthly
- Break down the cage completely, remove and discard particulate substrates.

- Sterilize drip containers and similar equipment in a mild bleach solution.

- Measure and weigh your lizard.

- Photograph your pet (recommended, but not imperative).

- Prune any plants present in the enclosure as necessary.

Annually
- Replace the batteries in your thermometers and any other devices that use them.

Cleaning your lizard's cage and furniture is relatively simple. Regardless of the way it became soiled, the basic process remains the same:

1. Rinse the object
2. Using a scrub brush or sponge and soapy water, remove any organic debris from the object.
3. Rinse the object thoroughly.
4. Disinfect the object.
5. Re-rinse the object.
6. Dry the object.

Chemicals & Tools
A variety of chemicals and tools are necessary for reptile care. Save yourself some time by purchasing dedicated cleaning products and keeping them in the same place that you keep your tools.

Spray Bottles
Occasionally misting your lizard's cage will help ensure the enclosure doesn't become too dry. You can do this with a small, handheld misting bottle or a larger, pressurized unit (such as those used to spray herbicides). Automated units are available, but they are rarely cost-effective unless you are caring for a large colony of animals.

Small Brooms

Small brooms are great for sweeping up small messes and bits of substrate. It is usually helpful to select one that features angled bristles, as they'll allow you to better reach the nooks and crannies of your pet's cage and the surrounding area.

Ideally, the broom should come with its own dustpan to collect debris, but there are plenty of workarounds for those that don't come with their own.

Scrub Brushes or Sponges

It helps to have a few different types of scrub brushes and sponges on hand for scrubbing and cleaning different items. Use the least abrasive sponge or brush suitable for the task to prevent wearing out cage items prematurely. Do not use abrasive materials on glass or acrylic surfaces. Steel-bristled brushes work well for scrubbing coarse, wooden items, such as branches.

Spatulas and Putty Knives

Spatulas, putty knives and similar tools are often helpful for cleaning reptile cages. For example, urates (which are not soluble in anything short of hot lava) often become stuck on cage walls or furniture. Instead of trying to dissolve them with harsh chemicals, just scrape them away with a sturdy plastic putty knife.

Small Vacuums

Small, handheld vacuums are very helpful for sucking up the dust left behind from substrates. They are also helpful for cleaning the cracks and crevices around the cage doors. A shop vacuum, with suitable hoses and attachments, can also be helpful if you have enough room to store it.

Soap

Use a gentle, non-scented dish soap. Antibacterial soap is preferred, but not necessary. Most people use far more soap than is necessary - - a few drops mixed with a quantity of water is usually sufficient to help remove surface pollutants.

Bleach

Bleach (diluted to one-half cup per gallon of water) makes an excellent disinfectant. Be careful not to spill any on clothing, carpets or furniture, as it is likely to discolor the objects.

Always be sure to rinse objects thoroughly after using bleach and be sure that you cannot detect any residual odor. Bleach does not work as a disinfectant when in contact with organic substances; accordingly, items must be cleaned before you can disinfect them.

Veterinarian Approved Disinfectant
Many commercial products are available that are designed to be safe for their pets. Consult with your veterinarian about the best product for your situation, its method of use and its proper dilution.

Avoid Phenols
Always avoid cleaners that contain phenols, as they are extremely toxic to some reptiles. In general, do not use household cleaning products to avoid exposing your pet to toxic chemicals.

Keeping Records
It is important to keep records regarding your pet's health, growth and feeding, as well as any other important details. In the past, reptile keepers would do so on small index cards or in a notebook. In the modern world, technological solutions may be easier.

You can record as much information about your pet as you like, and the more information to you record, the better. But minimally, you should record the following:

Pedigree and Origin Information
Be sure to record the source of your lizard, the date on which you acquired him and any other data that is available.

Breeders will often provide customers with information regarding the sire, dam, date of birth, weights and feeding records, but other sources will rarely offer comparable data.

Feeding Information
Record the date of each feeding, as well as the type of food item(s) offered. It is also helpful to record any preferences you may observe or any meals that are refused.

Weights and Length
Because you look at your pet frequently, it is difficult to appreciate how quickly he is (or isn't) growing. Accordingly, it is important to track his size diligently.

Weigh your pet with a high-quality digital scale. It is often easiest to use a dedicated "weighing container" with a known weight to measure your pet. Simply subtract the weight of the container to obtain the weight of your lizard.

You can also measure your lizard's length as well, but it is not always easy to do so – lizards tend to wiggle quite a bit, which can make it difficult to keep them in a straight line without putting undo pressure on their body.

However, there are a number of web-based computer applications that will calculate the length of your lizard if you take and upload a photo of him along with something of a known length (such as a ruler).

Maintenance Information
Record all of the noteworthy events associated with your pet's care. While it is not necessary to note that you misted the cage every other day, it is appropriate to record the dates on which you changed the substrate or sterilized the cage.

Whenever you purchase new equipment, supplies or caging, note the date and source. This not only helps to remind you when you purchased the items, but it may help you track down a source for the items in the future, if necessary.

Breeding Information
If you intend to breed your lizard, you should record all details associated with pre-breeding conditioning, cycling, introductions, matings, color changes, copulations and egg deposition.

Record all pertinent information about any resulting clutches as well, including the number of viable eggs, as well as the number of unhatched and unfertilized eggs.

Chapter 12: Feeding Lizards

For new keepers, few aspects of lizard care are as exciting as feeding their pet. However, feeding your pet properly entails more than just purchasing food items and tossing them in your lizard's cage periodically.

Instead, you must select the items you offer carefully, present them in a safe manner, and offer them on an appropriate schedule.

Types of Food

Different lizard species require different types of food. Some species will subsist entirely on plant matter, while others require live prey, ranging from insects to rodents or other vertebrates. Many species require both plant matter and animal-based foods.

You'll simply need to research the proper diet for the species you choose to keep. But we'll explain the basics of each type of food and how to provide it to your lizard below.

Fruits and Vegetables

Dark leafy greens are the best vegetables to offer most herbivorous and omnivorous lizards.

Some of the best leafy greens to provide include:

- Collard greens

- Turnip greens

- Mustard greens

- Dandelion greens

- Grape leaves

- Cilantro

- Parsley

- Kale

In addition to leafy greens, it is also wise to provide most omnivorous and herbivorous lizards with a number of other fruits and vegetables too.

Some of the best choices include:

- Broccoli

- Carrots

- Squash

- Zucchini

- Pumpkin

- Kiwi

- Strawberries

- Blueberries

- Blackberries

- Apples

- Pears

- Green beans

- Mango

- Grapes

- Melon

Edible roses and flowers, such as roses and hibiscus, can also be included in your lizard's diet, and they are often relished by many species.

Insects

Insects are another important food source for many lizards. Even some species that are often labelled as herbivorous can benefit from the occasional insect.

The following insects are some of the best choices for feeding lizards:

- Crickets

- Roaches

- Mealworms

- Giant mealworms

- Superworms

- Wax worms

- Grasshoppers

Vertebrates

In addition to vegetable matter or insects, many lizard species also require vertebrate prey.

The majority of commonly kept species will accept rodents as a source of vertebrate prey, but others may require chicks, crickets, fish, frogs or snakes.

Generally speaking, you should always opt for rodents whenever possible. They are the easiest to obtain, they are the least likely prey type to infect your lizard with parasites, and their fur help to firm up the feces the lizard will produce.

If you must offer your lizard another type of prey, always opt for captive-bred feeders whenever possible. This will help reduce the chances that your lizard will acquire parasites.

Chicks (or hatchling ducks) are likely the second-best option for lizards who will not need rodents.

Frogs, fish and other lizards are typically the most likely animals to transmit parasites to your pet, but you may have little choice.

How to Offer Food

Fruits and vegetables should be offered on a plate, dish or flat, clean rock. Always wash all fruits and vegetables before offering them to your pet, to help remove any waxes or pesticides, and be sure to cut them into small pieces to make it easier for your lizard to eat them.

You can simply release crickets and other insects into your pet's cage. This will also provide exercise and mental stimulation for your

pet. However, it is often better to place burrowing insects –
mealworms, roaches, etc. – on a feeding dish so that they do not
tunnel out of sight.

Do not allow large numbers of feeder insects to roam the enclosure
freely, as it can stress your pet. Additionally, the crickets may feed
on your lizard's delicate skin near his eyes and vent.

Feeding Frequency
The proper feeding frequency for your lizard depends on his size,
species and age. Generally speaking, most lizards should be fed four
to seven times per week; the younger the lizard, the more often it
should be fed.

As long as your lizard is healthy, gets plenty of exercise, has access
to suitable temperatures and is provided with a wide variety of food
items, you do not have to worry about over-feeding most species
during the first few years of life. However, mature animals – or
those living in small cages – may become overweight if fed too
frequently.

Ultimately, you must adjust your lizard's diet by monitoring his
weight regularly. Young lizards should exhibit steady, moderate
growth rates, while mature animals should maintain a relatively
consistent body weight.

If your lizard begins losing weight, you must increase the frequency
of his feedings. Conversely, those that gain excessive wait should be
placed on restrictive diets. Consult with your veterinarian before
altering your feeding schedule drastically.

Vitamin and Mineral Supplements
Many keepers add commercially produced vitamin and mineral
supplements to their lizard's food on a regular basis. In theory, these
supplements help to correct dietary deficiencies and ensure that
captive lizards get a balanced diet. In practice, things are not this
simple.

While some vitamins and minerals are unlikely to build up to toxic
levels, others may very well cause problems if provided in excess.
This means that you cannot simply apply supplements to every meal
– you must decide upon a sensible supplementation schedule.

Additionally, it can be difficult to ascertain exactly how much of the various vitamins and minerals you will be providing to your lizard, as most such products are sold as fine powders, designed to be sprinkled on feeder insects or vegetables.

This is hardly a precise way to provide the proper dose to your lizard, and the potential for grossly over- or under-estimating the amount of supplement delivered is very real.

Because the age, sex and health of your lizard all influence the amount of vitamins and minerals your pet requires, and each individual product has a unique composition, it is wise to consult your veterinarian before deciding upon a supplementation schedule.

However, most keepers provide vitamin supplementation once each week, and calcium supplementation several times per week.

Chapter 13: Providing Water to Your Lizard

Like most other animals, lizards require drinking water to remain healthy. And while providing drinking water is a fairly straightforward task, there are a few things to keep in mind while doing so.

Providing Drinking Water

Many lizards will readily drink water from a dish or bowl, but others prefer to acquire their drinking water by lapping up droplets of water that collect on leaves and grasses in their habitat. Some others will only drink water that is in motion or dripping down from above.

You can provide water to droplet drinkers by misting the habitat every morning with a bit of room-temperature water. Be sure to mist everything, including the lizard, the habitat walls and the branches and leaves in the enclosure.

For those species that prefer dripping water, a drip-system is the best way to provide water. Do not place ice cubes on top of the enclosure, as the resulting water is too cold for your lizard to drink.

However, it is still wise to provide droplet-drinking lizards with a dish full of clean, fresh drinking water at all times. This way, your lizard will always have access to water, even after the habitat has dried following the morning misting.

While it is acceptable to offer your pet a bowl that will accommodate his entire body, it is not necessary in most cases. Just be sure to avoid filling large containers too high, if you do so, as they are apt to overflow if the lizard crawls into the bowl.

Be sure to check the water dish daily and ensure that the water is clean. Empty, wash and refill the water dish any time it becomes contaminated with substrate, shed skin, urates or feces.

Some keepers prefer to use dechlorinated or bottled water for their lizards; however, untreated tap water is used by many keepers with no ill effects.

Soaking Lizards

In addition to providing drinking water, many keepers soak their lizard periodically in a tub of clean, lukewarm water. Soaking is helpful tool for the husbandry of many reptiles, and it helps to ensure proper hydration.

Additionally, soaks help to remove dirt and encourage complete, problem-free sheds. It is not necessary to soak your lizard if it remains adequately hydrated, but most will benefit from an occasional soak.

Soaks should last a maximum of about one hour and be performed no more often than once per week (unless the lizard is experiencing shedding difficulties).

When soaking your lizard, the water should not be very deep. Never make your lizard swim to keep its head above water.

Ideally, lizards should be soaked in containers with only enough water to cover their backs. This should allow your lizard to rest comfortably with its head above water.

Green iguanas require very large habitats in captivity.

It is important to monitor your lizard while he is soaking -- never leave a pet unattended while he is in a container of water. If your lizard defecates in the water, be sure to rinse him off with clean water before returning him to his cage.

Chapter 14: Interacting with Your Lizard

Many keepers enjoy handling pet lizards; assuming that they do not occur too frequently, gentle, brief handling sessions will rarely cause your pet much distress.

However, some lizards are a little more easily stressed than others, so you'll want to adjust the amount of interaction you engage in with your lizard to suit his personality.

Nevertheless, it will be necessary to handle your lizard from time to time – not only so that you can move your pet when it becomes necessary to clean the cage, but also to monitor its health.

Every lizard is an individual, which means that different lizards respond differently when interacting with their keeper.

Nevertheless, most captive raised lizards learn to tolerate gentle handling, although some remain nervous throughout their lives.

No matter what side of the spectrum your lizard falls on, you must be able to handle your pet when necessary.

Lifting a Lizard

Try to move with a purpose once you open the cage door. Don't stare at your lizard for 15 minutes as you try to work up your nerve. This often makes lizards feel insecure and increases their stress level.

Pick up your lizard by gently sliding your fingers underneath it and lifting its entire body into the air. Small lizards can be supported adequately with one hand, but two hands are necessary for lifting larger specimens.

Holding a Lizard

Now that you have picked up your lizard, you must hold him in a way that prevents stress or injury.

The best way to hold a lizard and keep it from feeling threatened is to provide it with plenty of support and allow it to crawl freely through your hands.

Avoid restraining your lizard or gripping it tightly with your hands, as this will cause it to feel like prey. Instead, simply support its body weight, and allow it to crawl from one hand to the other.

It is always wise to handle the lizard over a table or other object to prevent his from falling to the floor, should he make a sudden move.

Transporting Your Pet

Although you should strive to avoid any unnecessary travel with your lizard, circumstances (such as illness) may demand that you do. Strive to make the journey as stress-free as possible for your pet. This means protecting him from physical harm, as well as blocking out any stressful stimuli.

The best type of container to use when transporting your lizard is a plastic storage box. Add several ventilation holes to the container to provide suitable air exchange and be sure that the lid fits securely.

Place a few paper towels or some clean newspaper in the bottom of the box in case your lizard defecates or discharges urates. It is also wise to crumple a few of the layers of newspaper, which will provide a place in which your lizard can hide.

Cover the outside of the transport cage if you are not using an opaque container, which will prevent your pet from seeing the chaos occurring outside his container. Check up on your lizard regularly but avoid constantly opening the container to take a peak. A quick peak once every half-hour or so is sufficient.

Pay special attention to the enclosure temperatures while traveling. Use your digital thermometer to monitor the air temperatures inside the transportation container. Try to keep the temperatures in the mid-70s Fahrenheit (23 to 25 degrees Celsius) so that your pet will remain comfortable.

Use the air-conditioning or heater in your vehicle as needed to keep the transport cage within this range (because you cannot control the thermal environment, it is not wise to take your lizard with you on public transportation).

Keep your lizard's transportation container stable while traveling. Do not jostle the container unnecessarily and always use a gentle touch when moving it. Never leave the container unattended.

Hygiene

Reptiles can carry *Salmonella* spp., *Escherichia coli* and several other zoonotic pathogens and parasites.

Accordingly, it is imperative to use good hygiene practices when handling reptiles. Always wash your hands with soap and warm water each time you touch your pet, his habitat or the tools you use to care for him. Antibacterial soaps are preferred, but standard hand soap will suffice.

In addition to keeping your hands clean, you must also take steps to ensure your environment does not become contaminated with pathogens. In general, this means keeping your lizard and any of the tools and equipment you use to maintain his habitat separated from your belongings.

Establish a safe place to prepare your pet's food, store equipment and clean his habitat. Make sure the place is far from places human food is prepared. Never wash cages or tools in kitchens or bathrooms that are used by humans. Always clean and sterilize any items that become contaminated by the germs from your lizard or his habitat.

Chapter 15: Common Health Concerns

Like many other reptiles, most lizards are remarkably hardy animals, who often remain healthy despite their keeper's mistakes. In fact, most illnesses that befall pet lizards result from improper husbandry, and are, therefore, entirely avoidable.

Nevertheless, like most other reptiles, lizards often fail to exhibit any symptoms that they are sick until they have reached an advanced state of illness. This means that prompt action is necessary at the first hint of a problem. Doing so provides your pet with the greatest chance of recovery.

While proper husbandry is solely in the domain of the keeper, and some minor injuries or illnesses can be treated at home, veterinary care is necessary for many health problems.

Finding a Suitable Vet

While any veterinarian – even one who specializes in dogs and cats – may be able to help you keep your pet happy, it is wise to find a veterinarian who specializes in treating reptiles. Such veterinarians are more likely to be familiar with your pet species and be familiar with the most current treatment standards for reptiles.

Some of the best places to begin your search for a reptile-oriented veterinarian include:

- Veterinary associations

- Local pet stores

- Local colleges and universities

It is always wise to develop a relationship with a qualified veterinarian before you need his or her services. This way, you will already know where to go in the event of an emergency, and your veterinarian will have developed some familiarity with your pet.

When to See the Vet

Most conscientious keepers will not hesitate to seek veterinary attention on behalf of their pet. However, veterinary care can be expensive for the keeper and stressful for the kept, so unnecessary visits are best avoided.

If you are in doubt, call or email your veterinarian and explain the problem. He or she can then advise you if the problem requires an office visit or not.

However, you must always seek prompt veterinary care if your pet exhibits any of the following signs or symptoms:

- Traumatic injuries, such as lacerations, burns, broken bones or puncture wounds

- Sores, ulcers, lumps or other deformations of the skin

- Intestinal disturbances that do not resolve within 48 hours

- Drastic change in behavior

- Inability to deposit eggs

Remember that reptiles are perfectly capable of feeling pain and suffering, so apply the golden rule: If you would appreciate medical care for an injury or illness, it is likely that your pet does as well.

Common Health Problems

The following are some of the most common health problems that afflict lizards. Be alert for any signs of the following maladies and take steps to remedy the problem.

Respiratory Infections

Respiratory infections are some of the most common illnesses that afflict lizards and other captive reptiles.

The most common symptoms of respiratory infections are discharges from the nose or mouth; however, lethargy, inappetence and behavioral changes (such as basking more often than normal) may also accompany respiratory infections.

Myriad causes can lead to this type of illness, including communicable pathogens, as well as, ubiquitous, yet normally harmless, pathogens, which opportunistically infect stressed animals.

Your lizard may be able to fight off these infections without veterinary assistance, but it is wise to solicit your vet's opinion at the first sign of illness. Some respiratory infections can prove fatal and require immediate attention.

Your vet will likely obtain samples, send off the samples for laboratory testing and then interpret the results. Antibiotics or other medications may be prescribed to help your lizard recover, and your veterinarian will likely encourage you to keep the pet's stress level low and ensure his enclosure temperatures are ideal.

In fact, it is usually a good idea to raise the temperature of the basking spot upon first suspecting that your lizard is suffering from a respiratory infection. Elevated body temperatures (such as those that occur when mammals have fevers) help the pet's body to fight the infection, and many will bask for longer than normal when ill.

Internal Parasites
In the wild, most lizards carry some internal parasites. While it may not be possible to keep a lizard completely free of internal parasites, it is important to keep these levels in check.

Consider any wild-caught lizard to be parasitized until proven otherwise. While most captive bred lizards should have relatively few internal parasites, they can suffer from such problems as well.

Most internal parasites that are of importance for lizards are transmitted via the fecal-oral route. This means that eggs (or similar life stages) of the parasites are released with the feces. If the lizard inadvertently ingests these, the resulting parasites can develop inside the lizard's body and cause illness.

Such eggs are usually microscopic and easily lifted into the air, where they may stick to cage walls or land in the water dish. Later, when the lizard flicks its tongue or drinks from the water dish, it ingests the eggs.

Because cages that are continuously contaminated from feces are likely to lead to dangerous parasite loads, always employ strict hygiene practices.

Internal parasites may cause your lizard to vomit, pass loose stools, fail to grow or refuse food entirely. Other parasites may produce no symptoms at all, which illustrates the importance of routine examinations.

Your veterinarian will usually examine your lizard's feces if he suspects internal parasites. By looking at the type of eggs inside the lizard's feces, you veterinarian can determine which medication will treat the problem.

Many parasites are easily treated with anti-parasitic medications, but often, these medications must be given several times to eradicate the pathogens completely.

Some parasites may be transmissible to people, so always take proper precautions, including regular hand washing and keeping lizards and their cages away from kitchens and other areas where foods are prepared.

Examples of common internal parasites include roundworms, tapeworms and amoebas.

"Mouth Rot"

Mouth rot – properly called stomatitis – can be identified by noting discoloration, discharge or cheesy-looking material in the lizard's mouth. Mouth rot can be a serious illness and requires the attention of your veterinarian.

While mouth rot often follows injury (such as happens when a lizard bangs into the side of a glass cage) it can also arise from systemic illness. Your veterinarian will cleanse your lizard's mouth and potentially prescribe an antibiotic.

Your veterinarian may recommend withholding food until the problem is remedied. Always be sure that lizards that are recovering from mouth rot are kept in immaculately clean habitats with ideal temperature gradients.

External Parasites

The primary external parasites that afflict lizards are ticks and mites. Ticks are rare on captive bred animals, but wild caught lizards may be plagued by dozens of the small arachnids.

Ticks should be removed manually. Using tweezers grasp the tick as close as possible to the lizard's skin and pull with steady, gentle pressure. Do not place anything over the tick first, such as petroleum jelly, or carry out any other "home remedies," such as burning the tick with a match. Such techniques may cause the tick to inject more saliva (which may contain diseases or bacteria) into the lizard's body.

Drop the tick in a jar of isopropyl alcohol to kill it. It is a good idea to bring these to your veterinarian for analysis. Do not contact ticks with your bare hands, as many species can transmit disease to humans.

Mites are another matter entirely. While ticks are generally large enough to see easily, mites are about the size of a pepper flake. Whereas very bad tick infestations number in the dozens, mite infestations may include thousands of individual parasites.

Mites may afflict wild caught lizards, but, as they are not confined to a small cage, such infestations are somewhat self-limiting. In captivity, mite infestations can approach plague proportions.

After a female mite feeds on a lizard, she drops off and finds a safe place (such as a tiny crack in a cage or among the substrate) to deposit her eggs. After the eggs hatch, they travel back to your lizard (or to other lizards in your collection) where they feed and perpetuate the lifecycle.

Whereas a few mites may represent little more than an inconvenience to the lizard, significant infestations can stress them considerably. In extreme cases, they may even lead to anemia and eventual death. This is particularly true for small or young animals. Additionally, mites may transmit disease from one lizard to another.

There are a number of different methods for eradicating a mite infestation. In each case, there are two primary steps that must be taken: You must eradicate the lizard's parasites and eradicate the parasites in the lizard's environment (which includes the room in which the cage resides).

It is relatively simple to remove mites from a lizard. When mites get wet, they die. However, mites are protected by a thick, waxy exoskeleton that stimulates the formation of an air bubble.

To defeat this waxy cuticle, you can simply add a few drops of liquid soap to the water. The soap will lower the surface tension of water, thereby preventing the air bubble from forming.

Soaking your lizard is the slightly soapy water for about one hour will kill most of the mites on his body. Use care when doing so but try to arrange the water level and container so that most of the lizard's body is below the water.

While the lizard is soaking, perform a thorough cage cleaning. Remove everything from the cage, including water dishes, substrates and cage props. Sterilize all impermeable cage items and discard the substrate and all porous cage props. Vacuum the area around the cage and wipe down all of the nearby surfaces with a wet cloth.

It may be necessary to repeat this process several times to eradicate the mites completely. Accordingly, the very best strategy is to avoid contracting mites in the first place. This is why it is important to purchase your lizard from a reliable breeder or retailer, and keep it quarantined from potential mite vectors.

Even if you purchase your lizard from a reliable source, provide excellent husbandry and clean the cage regularly, you can end up battling mites if your friend brings his lizard – which has a few mites – to your house.

It may even be possible for mites to crawl onto your hands or clothes, hop off when you return home and make their way to your lizard.

Make it a practice to inspect your lizard and his cage regularly. Look in the crease under the lizard's lower jaw, near the eyes and near the vent -- common places in which mites hide. It can also be helpful to wipe down your lizard with a damp, white paper towel. After wiping down the lizard, observe the towel to see if any mites are present.

Chemical treatments are also available to combat mites, but you must be very careful with such substances. Beginners should rely on their veterinarian to prescribe or suggest the appropriate products to use.

Avoid repurposing lice treatments or other chemicals, as is often encouraged by other hobbyists. Such non-intended use may be very dangerous, and it is often in violation of Federal laws.

New hobbyists should consult with their veterinarian if they suspect that their lizard has mites. Mite eradication is often a challenging ordeal that your veterinarian can help make easier.

Long-Term Anorexia
While short-term fasts are common among some lizards, those that last for a long time are cause for concern. If your lizard refuses food, ensure that its habitat is set up ideally with ample hiding opportunities and access to appropriate temperatures.

If none of these factors requires attention, consult your veterinarian.

Your veterinarian will want to make sure that your lizard is in good health, as respiratory infections, mouth rot or internal parasites may cause him to refuse food.

Some lizards refuse food in the winter or breeding season, as they would in the wild. While you should consult with your veterinarian the first time this happens, it shouldn't cause you much concern in subsequent years.

Injuries
Lizards can become injured in myriad ways. While they are likely to heal from most minor wounds without medical attention, serious wounds will necessitate veterinary assistance.

Your vet will likely clean the wound, make any repairs necessary and prescribe a course of antibiotics to help prevent infection. Be sure to keep the enclosure as clean as possible during the healing process.

Egg Binding

Egg binding occurs when a female is unable or unwilling to deposit her eggs in a timely fashion. If not treated promptly, death can result.

The primary symptoms of egg binding are similar to those that occur when a gravid lizard approaches parturition. Egg bound lizards may explore their egg deposition chamber incessantly or attempt to escape their enclosure. However, unlike lizards who will deposit eggs normally, egg bound lizards continue to exhibit these symptoms without producing a clutch of eggs.

As long as you are expecting your lizard to lay eggs, you can easily monitor her behavior and act quickly if she experiences problems. However, if you are not anticipating a clutch, this type of problem can catch you by surprise.

Prolapse

Prolapses occur when a lizard's intestines protrude from its vent. This is an emergency situation that requires prompt treatment. Fortunately, intestinal prolapse is not terribly common among lizards.

You will need to take the animal to the veterinarian, who will attempt to re-insert the intestinal sections. Sometimes sutures will be necessary to keep the intestines in place while the muscles regain their tone.

Try to keep the exposed tissue damp, clean and protected while traveling to the vet. It is likely that this problem is very painful for the animal, so try to keep its stress level low during the process.

Quarantine

Quarantine is the practice of isolating animals to prevent them from transferring diseases between themselves.

If you have no other pet reptiles (particularly other lizards), quarantine is unnecessary. However, if you already maintain other lizards of the same species, you must provide all new acquisitions with a separate enclosure.

At a minimum, quarantine all new acquisitions for 30 days. However, it is wiser still to extend the quarantine period for 60 to 90 days, to give yourself a better chance of discovering any illness present before exposing your colony to new, potentially sick, animals. Professional zoological institutions often quarantine animals for six months to a year. In fact, some zoos keep their animals in a state of perpetual quarantine.

Chapter 16: Breeding Lizards

Many lizard keepers are intrigued at the idea of breeding their pets. While this is a fun, educational activity, you must be sure that you understand the risks and responsibilities that accompany such attempts.

For example, it is often necessary to allow your lizard to brumate to instigate breeding behaviors. Exposing your animal to reduced temperatures makes them more susceptible to illness. When their body temperatures are low, lizards' immune systems do not work as effectively as normal. If your lizards become sick during the brumation period, they will require immediate veterinary attention.

Other problems may occur as well; males may suffer damaged hemipenes or females may become egg bound. Either of which may be fatal without prompt treatment. You may find it necessary to take your pet to the veterinarian for costly treatment – potentially without any guarantee of success.

If you manage to get through the entire process without problem, you may one day find eggs that require incubation. If this is successful, you will find yourself caring for a dozen or more other lizards. Conversely, if you decide to work with a live-bearing species, you'll need to care for the gravid female and the neonates that are eventually produced.

And while it is possible to sell these young lizards, this is not as easy as it sounds, and it rarely generates profit.

Many municipalities require expensive permits to keep large numbers of reptiles – selling them requires other permits altogether.

You will have to learn how to ship lizards and obtain the necessary permits for that. Additionally, you will have to spend money to advertise that you have lizards for sale. Ultimately, most beginners find that it is simply best to give away the reptiles to other keepers.

You must also consider the costs associated with housing a large number of neonate lizards. Each will need its own habitat, heat supply and water dish, as most species should not be housed together.

Pre-Cycling Conditioning

Only lizards in perfect health should be considered for breeding trials. If a lizard exhibits signs of stress, respiratory illness, mites, mouth rot or other illnesses, avoid breeding the lizard or engaging in cycling until it is 100 percent healthy.

During the late summer and early fall, feed adults slated for breeding trials heavily. However, avoid allowing either animal to become overweight – overweight lizards make poor breeders.

Thermal- and Photo-Cycling

Before describing a generalized cycling process, it is important to note that some lizards will successfully breed without the need for cycling. Many equatorial species, for example, will breed readily when provided with consistent temperatures and photoperiods all year long.

But, most breeders employ a thermal- and photo-cycle that fluctuates throughout the year – even if the species they work with does not need to be cycled. If nothing else, it likely helps to synchronize the breeding pairs.

Different lizards require different cycling regimens, but the following represents a generalized example:

Stop feeding the animals in late autumn, while the cage temperatures are still at their normal levels. After at least two weeks have passed, and the lizards have had time to empty their digestive system completely, you can gradually begin lowering the cage temperature. It can also be helpful to reduce the relative day-length, as happens in the wild.

For tropical species, you need only drop the temperatures a handful of degrees. You may even want to continue providing warm days, and simply drop the nighttime temperatures.

Others, however, require a true "winter," which will induce brumation, with temperatures hovering in the 50- to 60-degree-Fahrenheit range (10 to 15 degrees Celsius).

Most often, this entails turning the heating devices off completely and allowing the temperatures to fall. Usually the lizards will become essentially dormant, although they may move about from time to time, drink water or respond to stimuli.

Often, it is necessary to move the cage (or use a separate brumation container) to another location to achieve the proper temperatures. For instance, garages, storage rooms and other places may dip into the 50s Fahrenheit, offering more appropriate temperatures than a living room or bedroom.

The length of brumation varies, but in general, two months is the approximate amount of time necessary. After this, you can gradually increase the temperatures until they are back to normal.

Once your lizards have been warm for a few days, you can consider feeding them, although many will refuse food.

Pairing

As soon as the lizards have been brought back up to the correct temperatures, they are ready to begin introducing to each other.

It is always wise to observe lizards when you introduce them to each other – particularly when it is the first time two individuals have met. Some lizards just are not compatible and may engage in antagonistic behaviors or fight. This can lead to serious injuries or death if the subordinate animal cannot escape.

Some breeders prefer to place males in the females' cages, while others prefer the opposite. Still others use a neutral cage, unique to both.

Pairs may begin copulating minutes after you place them in the same cage, or they may never breed if they are not compatible. Generally, lizards are housed together until they copulate, and then they are separated and fed, if they will eat.

Reintroduce the lizards periodically to allow further mattings and increase the chances for fertile eggs. When the pair stops showing interest, halt the introductions.

Post-Partum Care and Egg Deposition

After several copulations, the female can be kept by herself and fed regularly. Always offer smaller-than-normal food items at this time, to reduce the chances of disrupting the reproductive processes.

If you're keeping an egg-laying species, you'll want to introduce an egg-laying box to the habitat after copulations have occurred.

The egg-laying box is similar to a hide box, but it includes some moss, mulch or newspaper in the bottom. Different breeders prefer different substrates for the box, but there is likely little difference between the various options.

The egg-laying medium should be very slightly damp, but not wet. Err on the side of dryness, to avoid problems with mold, bacteria and fungi.

If you are working with live-bearing species, you'll simply need to take good care of the mother and wait for her to give birth. You'll then have the chance to remove the babies.

Allow the female to rest and rehydrate for about 24 hours after depositing eggs or giving birth, and then offer her food. Most females eat ravenously at this time to help replenish their energy stores.

The Incubator

If you are working with an egg-laying species, you'll need an incubator of some type. You can either purchase a commercially produced incubator or construct your own. However, most beginning breeders are better served by purchasing a commercial incubator than making their own.

Commercial Incubators
Commercial egg incubators come in myriad styles and sizes. Some of the most popular models are similar to those used to incubate poultry eggs (these are often available for purchase from livestock supply retailers).

These incubators are constructed from a large foam box, fitted with a heating element and thermostat. Some models feature a fan for circulating air; while helpful for maintaining a uniform thermal environment, models that lack these fans are acceptable.

You can place an incubation medium directly in the bottom of these types of incubators, although it is preferable to place the media (and eggs) inside small plastic storage boxes, which are then placed inside the incubator.

These incubators are usually affordable and easy to use, although their foam-based construction makes them less durable than most premium incubators are.

Other incubators are constructed from metal or plastic boxes; feature a clear door, an enclosed heating element and a thermostat. Some units also feature a backup thermostat, which can provide some additional protection in case the primary thermostat fails.

These types of incubators usually outperform economy, foam-based models, but they also bear higher price tags. Either style will work, but, if you plan to breed lizards for many years, premium models usually present the best option.

Homemade Incubators
Although incubators can be constructed in a variety of ways, using many different materials and designs, two basic designs are most common.

The first type of homemade incubator consists of a plastic, glass or wood box, and a simple heat source, such as a piece of heat tape or a low-wattage heat lamp. The heating source must be attached to a thermostat to keep the temperatures consistent. A thermometer is also necessary for monitoring the temperatures of the incubator.

Some keepers make these types of incubators from wood, while others prefer plastic or foam. Although glass is a poor insulator, aquariums often serve as acceptable incubators; however, you must purchase or construct a solid top to retain heat.

Place a brick on the bottom of the incubator and place the egg box on top of the brick, so that the eggs are not resting directly on the heat tape. The brick will also provide thermal mass to the incubator, which will help maintain a more consistent temperature.

The other popular incubator design adds a quantity of water to the design to help maintain consistent temperatures and a higher humidity. To build such a unit, begin with an aquarium fitted with a glass or plastic lid.

Place a brick in the bottom of the aquarium and add about two gallons of water to the aquarium; ideally, the water level should stop right below the top of the brick.

Add an aquarium heater to the water and set the thermostat to the desired temperature. Place the egg box on the brick, insert a temperature probe into the egg box and cover the aquarium with the lid (you may need to purchase a lid designed to allow the cords to pass through it).

This type of incubator works by heating the water, which will in turn heat the air inside the incubator, which will heat the eggs. Although it can take several days of repeated adjustments to get these types of incubators set to the exact temperature you would like, they are very stable once established.

Incubating the Eggs

Plastic storage boxes are often used to hold the eggs during incubation. Fill the box half way with damp vermiculite. Ensure that the vermiculite is damp enough to clump, but not so damp that it drips when compressed. As a starting point, combine equal weights of water and vermiculite and then adjust the mixture as necessary. Make a few small holes in the incubation box to provide some air exchange.

Before removing the eggs from the egg-laying box, mark the top of each egg with a graphite pencil. This is necessary because the tiny lizard embryo attaches to the inside of the eggshell at an early stage in development. If the egg is rotated after this happens, the young animal can drown inside the egg.

After marking the tops, gently remove the eggs and transfer them to the egg incubation box. Do not use force to separate any eggs that are attached – while experienced breeders often separate such eggs, the risk of destroying some of them is high. Simply place clumps of attached eggs in the egg incubation box in the same orientation in which they are in the deposition box.

Place the eggs in the incubation box in the same orientation in which they were deposited in the egg-laying box. Bury the eggs about halfway in the vermiculite.

There are many different opinions regarding the best place to install the thermostat's temperature probe. Some prefer placing it in the main incubator chamber, while others prefer to place the probe inside the egg box.

Place the egg incubation box inside the incubator and close it tightly. Do not inspect the eggs too frequently, as this may cause unnecessary temperature spikes.

Lizard eggs exhibit a wide range of incubation durations, although most hatch in about 40 to 90 days. You can incubate most eggs at about 80 to 90 degrees Fahrenheit (26 to 32 degrees Celsius), although the ideal temperature range will vary from one species to the next.

Neonate Husbandry

Establish "nursery cages" for the young lizards about a week before the eggs should hatch or the mother is likely to give birth. The container should contain only a paper towel substrate, a very shallow water dish, some branches (for climbing species) and a few places to hide (crumpled newspaper works well).

Keep the nursery very clean, slightly humid and at about 80 to 86 degrees Fahrenheit (26 to 30 degrees Celsius), 24-hours a day. Do not handle the neonates unless necessary, until they are about one month old and eating well.

It is not uncommon for hatchlings to emerge from their eggs or their mother's body with their yolks still attached. Do not attempt to remove or separate the tissue in such situations; doing so could cause severe injury or death to the young lizards. Instead, simply keep the hatchling in a nursery cage and ensure that the tissue does not dry out. Generally, by keeping the nursery slightly humid, the tissue will remain moist and dethatch on in its own in a few days.

Chapter 17: Species Accounts

There may be more than 6,000 lizard species in the world, but only a handful of species make good pets.

We'll discuss five of the best choices below, so that you can make an informed decision before purchasing a lizard for a pet.

Leopard Gecko

Leopard geckos (*Eublepharis macularius*) are probably the most commonly kept lizard species in captivity, and it is easy to see why: They're not only easy to keep and attractive, they also have delightful personalities.

Leopard geckos reach about 8 to 11 inches (20 to 28 centimeters) in length, so they're pretty easy to house. Most will thrive in a habitat about the size of a 10- or 20-gallon aquarium. They will remain healthy on an insect-based diet, and most are tame enough to handle regularly.

Leopard geckos hail from dry regions of southwest Asia, where they live a predominantly nocturnal lifestyle. They've been bred in captivity for several decades, so it isn't hard for hobbyists to acquire captive-bred specimens. In fact, part of the reason that leopard geckos are so popular is the fact that they're available in several color and pattern varieties.

Bearded Dragon

Bearded dragons (*Pogona vitticeps*) are another popular lizard species among reptile keepers.

Unlike leopard geckos, bearded dragons are omnivores, who require plant- and animal-based foods to remain healthy. They're also diurnal animals, who have relatively specific lighting requirements that keepers will need to satisfy.

Bearded dragons are noteworthy for being rather docile animals, who rarely mind being handled by their keepers. In fact, they're one of the most common species used by wildlife educators, as they make excellent reptilian ambassadors.

Bearded dragons reach lengths of up to 24 inches (60 centimeters), so they require relatively large enclosures. Typically, keepers should strive to provide bearded dragons with 4- to 8-square feet of cage space.

Crested Gecko

Crested geckos (*Correlophus ciliatus*) haven't been available to hobbyists for as long as leopard geckos or bearded dragons (they were actually thought extinct for decades until they were rediscovered). However, they're quickly proving to be equally popular among keepers.

Crested geckos are small, nocturnal, tree-dwelling lizards. Part of the reason they're so popular among hobbyists is that they're very easy to care for. They are omnivorous in the wild, but they'll survive solely on a prepared diet (resembling baby food) in captivity.

Additionally, crested geckos rarely need heating devices, as they'll thrive at room temperature. Also, as they're nocturnal, they do not require any type of special lighting.

Uromastyx

Also called dab lizards, uromastyx lizards (*Uromastyx* spp.) are somewhat odd-looking animals, who have short, plump bodies and spiked tails. They hail from deserts in Africa and the Middle East, where they subsist on a variety of different foods, including vegetation and insects.

There are a variety of different uromastyx species available to hobbyists, so it is important for prospective keepers to research the needs of their particular pet to ensure they provide the lizard with the proper care.

Nevertheless, most uromastyx species require broadly similar care, and several species make very good pets. Most uromastyx are quite docile, and they make an interesting alternative to bearded dragons.

Green Iguana

For many years, the green iguana (*Iguana iguana*) was the most popular lizard species among reptile enthusiasts. But they no longer enjoy the popularity they once did, as hobbyists have learned that these lizards are somewhat difficult to care for.

For starters, green iguanas are very large animals, who may occasionally reach 6 feet (2 meters) in length. They also require very large enclosures, which are not only expensive to purchase, but challenging to heat as well.

Further, green iguanas can be challenging to feed, as they're essentially herbivorous, and they require specialized lighting in order to remain healthy. Finally, many green iguanas are foul-tempered animals, who don't enjoy being handled or interacting with their keepers.

Nevertheless, some keepers continue to enjoy these lizards, and they can make suitable pets for those willing to put in the necessary effort.

Chapter 18: Further Reading

Never stop learning more about your new pet's natural history, biology and captive care. This is the only way to ensure that you are providing your new lizard with the highest quality of life possible.

It's always more fun to watch your lizard than read about him, but by accumulating more knowledge, you'll be better able to provide him with a high quality of life.

Books

Bookstores and online book retailers offer a treasure trove of information that will advance your quest for knowledge. While books represent an additional cost involved in reptile care, you can consider it an investment in your pet's well-being. Your local library may also carry some books about lizards, which you can borrow for no charge.

University libraries are a great place for finding old, obscure or academically oriented books about lizards. You may not be allowed to borrow these books if you are not a student, but you can view and read them at the library.

Herpetology: An Introductory Biology of Amphibians and Reptiles
By Laurie J. Vitt, Janalee P. Caldwell
Top of Form
Bottom of Form
Academic Press, 2013

Understanding Reptile Parasites: A Basic Manual for Herpetoculturists & Veterinarians
By Roger Klingenberg D.V.M.
Advanced Vivarium Systems, 1997

Infectious Diseases and Pathology of Reptiles: Color Atlas and Text
Elliott Jacobson

CRC Press

Designer Reptiles and Amphibians
Richard D. Bartlett, Patricia Bartlett
Barron's Educational Series

Magazines
Because magazines are typically published monthly or bi-monthly, they occasionally offer more up-to-date information than books do. Magazine articles are obviously not as comprehensive as books typically are, but they still have considerable value.

Reptiles Magazine
www.reptilesmagazine.com/
Covering reptiles commonly kept in captivity.

Practical Reptile Keeping
http://www.practicalreptilekeeping.co.uk/
Practical Reptile Keeping is a popular publication aimed at beginning and advanced hobbies. Topics include the care and maintenance of popular reptiles as well as information on wild reptiles.

Websites
The internet has made it much easier to find information about reptiles than it has ever been.

However, you must use discretion when deciding which websites to trust. While knowledgeable breeders, keepers and academics operate some websites, many who maintain reptile-oriented websites lack the same dedication to scientific rigor.

Anyone with a computer and internet connection can launch a website and say virtually anything they want about lizards. Accordingly, as with all other research, consider the source of the information before making any husbandry decisions.

The Reptile Report
www.thereptilereport.com/

The Reptile Report is a news-aggregating website that accumulates interesting stories and features about reptiles from around the world.

Kingsnake.com
www.kingsnake.com
After starting as a small website for gray-banded kingsnake enthusiasts, Kingsnake.com has become one of the largest reptile-oriented portals in the hobby. The site features classified advertisements, a breeder directory, message forums and other resources.

The Vivarium and Aquarium News
www.vivariumnews.com/
The online version of the former print publication, The Vivarium and Aquarium News provides in-depth coverage of different reptiles and amphibians in a captive and wild context.

Journals
Journals are the primary place professional scientists turn when they need to learn about lizards. While they may not make light reading, hobbyists stand to learn a great deal from journals.

Herpetologica
www.hljournals.org/
Published by The Herpetologists' League, Herpetologica, and its companion publication, Herpetological Monographs cover all aspects of reptile and amphibian research.

Journal of Herpetology
www.ssarherps.org/
Produced by the Society for the Study of Reptiles and Amphibians, the Journal of Herpetology is a peer-reviewed publication covering a variety of reptile-related topics.

Copeia
www.asihcopeiaonline.org/
Copeia is published by the American Society of Ichthyologists and Herpetologists. A peer-reviewed journal, Copeia covers all aspects of the biology of reptiles, amphibians and fish.

Nature
www.nature.com/

Although Nature covers all aspects of the natural world, many issues contain information that lizard enthusiasts are sure to find interesting.

Supplies

You can obtain most of what you need to maintain lizards through your local pet store, big-box retailer or hardware store, but online retailers offer another option.

Just be sure that you consider the shipping costs for any purchase, to ensure you aren't "saving" yourself a few dollars on the product yet spending several more dollars to get the product delivered.

Big Apple Pet Supply
http://www.bigappleherp.com

Big Apple Pet Supply carries most common husbandry equipment, including heating devices, water dishes and substrates.

LLLReptile
http://www.lllreptile.com

LLL Reptile carries a wide variety of husbandry tools, heating devices, lighting products and more.

Doctors Foster and Smith
http://www.drsfostersmith.com

Foster and Smith is a veterinarian-owned retailer that supplies husbandry-related items to pet keepers.

Support Organizations

Sometimes, the best way to learn about lizards is to reach out to other keepers and breeders. Check out these organizations, and search for others in your geographic area.

The National Reptile & Amphibian Advisory Council
http://www.nraac.org/

The National Reptile & Amphibian Advisory Council seeks to educate the hobbyists, legislators and the public about reptile and amphibian related issues.

American Veterinary Medical Association
www.avma.org
The AVMA is a good place for Americans to turn if you are having trouble finding a suitable reptile veterinarian.

The World Veterinary Association
http://www.worldvet.org/
The World Veterinary Association is a good resource for finding suitable reptile veterinarians worldwide.

References

Abigail S. Tucker a, G. J. (2014). Evolution and developmental diversity of tooth regeneration. *Seminars in Cell & Developmental Biology*.

Almeida, M. L.-R.-F. (2006). Distribution of neuromuscular junctions in laryngeal and syringeal muscles in vertebrates.

Anderson, S. P. (2003). The Phylogenetic Definition of Reptilia. *Systematic Biology*.

Arnold, S. J. (1972). Species Densities of Predators and Their Prey. *The American Naturalist*.

Bergmann, P. J. (2008). A phylogenetic and functional approach to the study of the evolution of body shape in lizards (Squamata). *University of Massachusetts Amherst*.

Jeffrey C. Beane, S. P. (2013). Published by: The American Society of Ichthyologists and Herpetologists. *Copeia*.

Made in the USA
Coppell, TX
04 April 2023

15209614R00056